THE

CHRISTIAN HOME,

OR

Religion in the Family.

BY THE

Rev. JOSEPH A. COLLIER,

KINGSTON, N. Y.

AUTHOR OF "THE RIGHT WAY," (A PRIZE ESSAY.)

PHILADELPHIA:

PRESBYTERIAN BOARD OF PUBLICATION,

No. 821 Chestnut Street.

A prize of one hundred and seventy-five dollars was awarded to the author of this work, by the Board of Publication of the Presbyterian Church.

STEREOTYPED BY JESPER HARDING & SON, PHILADELPHIA.

CONTENTS.

CHAPTER I.

THE FOUNDATION, NATURE, AND IMPORTANCE OF THE FAMILY CONSTITUTION.

CHAPTER II.

DUTIES AND RESPONSIBILITIES BELONGING TO THE FAMILY RELATION.

CHAPTER III.

PARENTAL DUTIES AND RESPONSIBILITIES, CONTINUED.

CHAPTER IV.

DUTIES OF CHILDREN TO THEIR PARENTS.

CHAPTER V.

DUTIES AND RESPONSIBILITIES OF MASTERS AND SERVANTS.

CHAPTER VI.

THE BEST MEANS OF SECURING THE END DESIGNED.

CHAPTER VII.

MEANS CONTINUED—PARENTAL PRAYER.

CHAPTER VIII.

THE RELATION OF THE FAMILY TO THE CHURCH.

CHAPTER IX.

THE VALUE, DIFFICULTIES, AND AIDS OF FAMILY RELIGION.

CHAPTER X.

PLEAS FOR NEGLECT AND DELINQUENCIES, DISCUSSED AND REFUTED.

THE CHRISTIAN HOME,

OR

RELIGION IN THE FAMILY.

CHAPTER I.

THE FOUNDATION, NATURE, AND IMPORTANCE OF THE FAMILY CONSTITUTION.

THE FAMILY! What word in our language is more suggestive of delightful associations, or more inwoven with the tenderest thoughts and emotions of the human heart? The loved home, the cheerful fireside group, the fond tones of a mother's voice, the sweet dependencies of childhood, the interchange of confiding sympathies, the community of joys and griefs, of hopes and fears—all unite in clothing it with surpassing interest, and in rendering it the scene to which, of all others upon earth, the mind best loves to revert. Even apart from the direct influences of religion, (for there is scarcely a home but feels those that are indirect,) it is beautiful indeed in its development of the kindlier affections of unsanctified humanity. What then must it be, when thoroughly pervaded by those holy principles that ally us to Divinity? Let there be added to its other attractions the charm of *piety;* let the mother's gentle voice be linked with memories of childhood's prayers, and the heart's first thoughts of heaven, until she seems an angel of the household, alluring us to the skies; let the law of Christian love bind heart to heart; let the family altar send up its daily incense, more sweet and grateful than the smoke of the ancient morning and evening sacrifice; and we have a scene which, in contrast with the waste, sin-desolated world without, is like an oasis in the desert, a garden in the wilderness. The *Christian* family is, or should be, the very type of heaven.

To promote *religion in the family*, therefore, which is the object of these pages, is to minister to the highest joys of which we are here susceptible, to add the crown of grace to that which is loveliest in nature, and to exalt and ennoble with heaven's own likeness the fairest scenes of earth. More than this, it is to promote religion in every sphere and relation of life; for the family is the basis of the social fabric, the foundation of the state, the empire, and the race. All will perceive that if the living streams of humanity are to be purified and made better, we can nowhere begin more appropriately than at these their fountains.

It is necessary, in order to a proper understanding of our subject, and a correct estimate of its magnitude, that we consider *the foundation, nature, and importance of the family constitution.*

I. Our first inquiry shall be, *upon what is it founded?*

We find it existing as an established institution, and so, in like manner, did our fathers find it. We trace it back through the history of the past, until we have gone beyond the rise of kingdoms, and even the visible organization of the church, and discover it to be the primal institution of the world, dating back its origin to the time of our first parents. It was appropriate that this relation, which is the holiest upon earth, should have been first formed in Eden, before the blight of sin had fallen upon our race. There was also a peculiar fitness in the fact of its appointment by the voice of God himself, uttered so plainly and authoritatively as to clothe it in all coming time with the sanctions of Divine, unchanging *law.* The account of its institution is contained in the second chapter of the book of Genesis, where we read that the first woman was formed out of a rib taken from Adam's side. Adam received the gift as bone of his bone, and flesh of his flesh; and God there ordained the sacred rite of marriage, in the words, "Therefore shall a man leave his father and his mother, and shall cleave unto his wife, and they twain shall be one flesh." "And God blessed them and God said unto them, Be fruitful, and multiply, and replenish the earth."

Thus, in *the Divine appointment* originated the family relation. It is not, like many lesser institutions, the invention of man, but, like the Sabbath, is ordained by God, and, like it, must ever retain the stamp of its great Author. "*He* setteth the solitary in families."

It is necessary that this fact be borne in mind as we proceed with our subject. For, that which is appointed by God rises immeasurably in importance above any thing that is of merely human device. It will also be seen that, if Divine in its origin, this relation must be Divine in its governing principles, and in the ends that it is intended to subserve; so that whatever be the lesser, temporary purposes of which it is the providential instrument, we are warranted in looking for higher ones, which are alike worthy of its Author, and promotive of man's best and everlasting interests. As the hand that formed the stars out of chaos has given to each one its appropriate orbit, so He who created man from the dust of the earth, has also ordained those endearing ties that unite the members of the family, and gather a certain number of individuals about the common fireside; and we must conclude that in the one instance, as in the other, this arrangement is intended to further the great object of all created existence, *the glory of God.*

It may be further remarked, that while the family relation is thus founded, primarily, upon the Divine appointment, it is also based, secondarily, upon *the necessities of mankind.* That God has seen fit to ordain it, is indeed a sufficient reason for its existence, and a warrant of its wisdom and beneficence. Yet as God's will always coincides with, or rather is itself, the highest wisdom, we may properly look for that within ourselves to which this institution is adapted, and which will furnish powerful reasons for its appointment. We shall see that it is, in a remarkable degree, answerable to the deepest wants and the highest aims of humanity; that while exactly suited to our physical and social condition in this world, it is also eminently calculated to promote our best moral and spiritual well being; and that, viewed in its grander aspect, from the stand-point of Bible truth, it occupies an important position in that remedial system which is intended to elevate the individual man, and finally to consummate the world's regeneration.

The *temporal ends* to be subserved by it, are so plain as to require only a passing notice. It is a well known fact that the human being is, of all others, the most helpless in infancy, as well as the longest dependent upon the kind offices of others. This providential circumstance goes far towards strengthening the tie that binds parent and child, and also affords the more ample opportunities for a thorough religious training. How wise is that provision which throws around the feeble child the tender, helpful influences of the family, and thus prepares it, in that gentler inner world, to grapple successfully with the realities of the sterner world without! And how beautiful are the adaptations of the family to all the great primary necessities of our nature! Infidel philosophy—flourishing the most luxuriantly in a land where the Christian family and the Anglo-Saxon home are scarcely known—has its theories of socialism, and community of labour, by which it would constitute families upon a human, instead of a Divine basis. Its signal failure is become matter of history. Its authors have blindly ignored the fact, which all experience sufficiently attests, that there is the truest philosophy in this relation *as constituted by God.* Here is the most admirable division of labour, combined with community of interest, that the world has ever seen. Here, too, are furnished the most constraining mutual obligations, and the most powerful motives to right conduct; while it is governed by the sanctions and penalties of Divine, unchanging law.

The same is true in regard to our needs *as social beings*. The ill-disguised libertinism of a certain class of reformers, "falsely so called," chafes, like a wayward child, under the wholesome restraints of the family relation. Perhaps the fact that it is assailed by such may be regarded as no slight proof of the wisdom that devised it. Yet it is impossible to conceive of any system so well calculated to develop our finer feelings in a way that shall ennoble, instead of degrading them, or that shall gratify our social instincts, and at the same time make them subservient to our higher and immortal interests. The sweet companionship of husband and wife, parents and children, brothers and sisters, when sanctified, as it was originally intended that it should be, by an all pervading piety, and hallowed fellowship with the Creator, certainly answers to the deepest cravings of the human heart, and satisfies them as they could be satisfied in no other way.

It is, however, when we rise to the consideration of its bearings upon our *moral welfare*, that we behold under its grandest aspect the family constitution. All are familiar with the thought that mankind is here in a state of pupilage; that every allotment of Providence, as well as every means of grace, has its part in the great disciplinary system by which God would educate the mind and heart for his service hereafter. This being the case, we might well conclude that so important a sphere as that of the family, cannot be without its bearings upon our character and destiny as moral beings.

If the world is a great school where the people of God are being trained for their inheritance, the family may be viewed as its *primary department.* It is, indeed, a mimic world in itself, where we may see reproduced in the history of the little child, the same emotions, passions, temptations, griefs, and joys, that agitate the bosom of manhood or old age. Who shall say that the tear dropped over a broken toy, or the word of anger lisped in childhood's accents, does not express feelings as deep and real as those vented in after years over a ruined fortune, or poured out in oaths and curses upon a fellow-man? In the same manner the generous self-sacrifice, the word of forgiving love, or the kind action, which scarcely attracts the attention of older persons, may thrill the young heart with emotions as truly noble as ever animated a Howard or a Martyn.

If this be so, it will be seen that no school is so favourable for the development of the higher affections as the Christian family. The outer world is not only a harsh disciplinarian, but its influence is rarely felt until habits have been in a measure formed, and the character has assumed a decided hue and shape. The family, upon the contrary, exerts its influence upon the open mind and heart of infancy. Whether its atmosphere be one of religion or irreligion, it is sure to be breathed with almost the first breath of life. Whether its culture be for the better or the worse, it has to deal, not with the gnarled and crooked tree, that hardly sways to the tempest, and whose roots are deeply bedded in the soil, but with the tender sapling, that is susceptible to gentlest influences, and capable of the highest cultivation.

Add to this the unbounded influence of parental affection and authority, when under proper regulation, the tender interest of each in the others' welfare, the often recurring opportunities for the exercise of every virtue and grace of piety, during a long course of years, and we have an aggregate of circumstances the most favourable to moral improvement of any that can be conceived. Now viewing man in his relations to the Creator, what is more evident than that we need precisely the sphere and the influences thus hinted at, and that as moral beings we could ill afford to be deprived of them?

We may contemplate this part of our subject in another light. The family constitution admirably *illustrates great spiritual truths*, and prepares the mind for their apprehension. That it is so intended by its Author is evident from the frequent allusions made to it in the word of God. Thus, he is our Father, and we are his children; the church is beautifully depicted as "the whole family in heaven and earth;" all believers are "brethren;" and heaven, after the same figure, is called our "Father's house," and our "inheritance." Says a distinguished writer, "The love in which the family constitution is founded, and all the deep affections which it develops and by which it is administered, are designed to aid man in the conception of the Fatherhood, the unknown benevolence of God towards his sinning human family, and in which the great promise of deliverance through the self-subordination and voluntary suffering of another, originated. The child obtains life, and all that makes life desirable, through another. Indeed the whole of parental duty is a system of *mediation*, often attended with suffering and self denial, but always impelled by love." * The subjection of the child to parental authority gives a point to the Divine upbraiding, "If I be a Father, where is mine honour?" and educates the heart for the submissive tribute, "Not my will but thine be done!" The path of loving filial obedience furnishes the best possible illustration of the cheerful service which alone is acceptable to God. The confiding trust of the child in the parent's loving protection, a trust that is often exercised blindly and in the dark, affords an insight into the important truth, "We walk by faith and not by sight." Indeed, were it not for the analogies thus afforded, it is difficult to imagine how man could be brought to realize his relations to his Maker.

Thus do both reason and experience unite in vindicating the wisdom of the family relation, and prove it to be founded in the most urgent necessities of our nature; thereby assigning to it a high place in those arrangements and adaptations of Providence which are working out the highest good of the creature, and the glory of the Creator.

II. Such being its broad and deep foundation, we may naturally look for a lofty and noble superstructure. Let us then contemplate more particularly ITS NATURE, as set forth in the teachings of its Author, and in the laws that govern it.

From these we learn that it is SACRED. We know not what the home of Adam would have been, had it been perpetuated in Paradise, but we may reasonably conclude that it would have been a scene that God and angels

---

* Harris's "Patriarchy."

would have loved to visit. Its joys would have been hallowed joys, and therefore unmixed with any sorrows. Its daily round of duties would have resembled the delightful service of the heavenly world. All its intercourse would have breathed the very spirit of love, while the virtues of forgiveness and forbearance—those flowers thrown by grace over nature's sad ruins—would have been unknown, because uncalled for. To crown all, it would have been blessed with the felt presence and audible benediction of the Creator, who would have condescended to hold converse with the happy group, even as He had walked with Adam "in the garden, in the cool of the day."

Such is the sacred character which the family was originally intended to possess. The thought that it *might have been* thus, renders yet more dark by contrast, the realities that so often cloud the domestic hearth. For now, alas! what forms of sin have degraded this sanctuary of the heart! How often God is banished from it, while all evil passions make it their dwelling place! Yet the fact that it was designed to be thus holy and heavenlike is a gladdening one; for if it is the Saviour's mission to repair the ruins of the fall, it follows that *the Christian family* may realize in kind, if not as yet in degree, the hallowed delights which this relation was intended to minister. When, under the renovating influences of the millennial era, this earth shall become a second paradise, the promise of the covenant, already verified in part, shall receive the grander fulfilment for which it has so long waited, "In thee shall *all the families* of the earth be blessed."

This view of the nature of the family institution is fully borne out by the Scriptures. Witness the many laws and precepts by which its duties are inculcated, and its rights vindicated. "The first commandment with promise" has relation to one class of obligations pertaining to it, and the Mosaic code embraces in its provisions many rules and regulations that bear directly upon it. The New Testament confirms the teachings of the Old upon this subject, and the whole inspired word unites to invest it with a dignity and sacredness which show, not only that it is *from* God, but also that, in its legitimate aims and ends, it tends *to* God.

Thus the Bible teaches us that it is sacred *in its obligations.* These are made a subject of express command; and its historic records unite with all experience in attesting that they are not to be violated with impunity. This is equally true of the lesser and more important duties; and where right views prevail, and the spirit of piety is actively present, the whole routine of household care and domestic intercourse will be more or less sanctified to holy ends. There is no duty of the home and fireside but may and should be hallowed by religion. Even those that appear the most insignificant may thus be clothed with dignity, and we may "eat and drink" around the family board "to the glory of God."

So, too, this relation is sacred *in its rights.* The claims of the parent upon the child, and of the child upon the parent; the mutual prerogatives of husband and wife, brother and sister, master and servant—all are guarded by divine laws, and vindicated by the weight of divine authority.

It is the same in *its ends*. The fact that it is ordained by God is a sufficient evidence that it is intended for the Divine glory. Subordinate to this, however, are certain lesser ends to which allusion has already been made—such as the fostering of our virtues and graces under circumstances the most favourable to their development, and the education of the young mind and heart in divine things. Perverted and abused this relationship may be, as is so frequently the case in the individual life, but its true end remains the same. Whether it be made the instrument of positive wrong and injustice, or simply subserve the end, so innocent in itself, of social happiness, it is, in either instance, degraded from its high purpose, and fails of fulfilling the intention of its Founder. It is the office of Christianity to elevate the aims and purposes of the family to their proper standard, to rescue it from the ignoble position to which human selfishness has lowered it, and to make it at the same time a powerful promoter of the Divine glory, and of man's best and highest good. "If the earth is a temple, the family is its 'holiest of all;' and all its divinely selected arrangements and influences are meant to be ever crying to each other, 'Holy, holy, holy is the Lord God Almighty,' as the continuous service of love and worship trains up its members for heaven."

It follows from what has been said that the family constitution is BINDING. Its duties, being imposed by the Ruler of the universe, and not by the mere voice of human authority, assume the importance of high moral obligations. We may not ask, with Cain, "Am I my brother's keeper?" nor may the parent, like Eli, withhold restraint from his erring children, without incurring positive and aggravated guilt. Whatever be the responsibilities involved in this relation, they are necessarily vast and momentous. Next to those duties which, as individuals, we all owe to God, or rather in inseparable connection with them, these of the family should be viewed as paramount. The nearness of the relationship involved, the tremendous bearings of our right or wrong conduct upon the common welfare, and the fact that this sphere of influence is especially assigned to us by God himself, who will require an account of our stewardship—all prove conclusively that these duties are the last to be trifled with, and that they bind us with a power of obligation from which nothing can absolve us.

There are those who appear greatly to misapprehend this truth, and who view the duties of the fireside as secondary to those pertaining to the world without. True Christian philanthropy is to be honoured, wherever met with, and under whatever circumstances; but surely it was never meant that it should be practised at the sacrifice of the dearest interests of the parental or filial heart. While it is true that our out-door deeds of kindness ought rather to be multiplied than diminished, the parent should yet feel that the claims of his child for instruction and spiritual training are far more imperative. It must be but a poor consolation to one whose offspring are reaping the bitter fruits of parental neglect, and treading paths of vice and crime, to reflect that the hand which should have arrested their downward course has fed the hungry or clothed the naked, and that the voice which should have counselled and admonished them has breathed kind words into the ear of sorrow.

Let it not, however, be inferred from this that faithfulness in the one sphere of duty necessitates any neglect of the other. Doubtless the proper method is to combine them both. The most consistent life is that which blends in beautiful symmetry the activities of the home, the church, and the world, neither of them conflicting with the others, but each promoting the efficiency of all the rest.

This relation is also strictly binding *in its ties.* How stringently does the word of God protect the union of husband and wife; not only guarding it against aught that could put it in peril, but declaring it *indissoluble,* except in instances of gross criminality! Our Saviour views it as a tie that is formed peculiarly by God, and which therefore, with the one exception already alluded to, is beyond the power of man to dissolve: "What therefore God hath joined together, let not man put asunder." The inspired writers exhibit the *Divine* estimate of the sanctity of the marriage relation, by employing it to illustrate the union of Christ to his church—a figure which would scarcely be appropriate, were either party at liberty to sever it upon slight cause.

It is, perhaps, scarcely worth while to notice in this connection the views of a class of social agitators of the present day, who are labouring to undermine this foundation of all society. We will only recur, in passing, to the well known fact that wherever this bond has been held in slight esteem, the curse of a just God has been vividly seen and felt, the flood-gates of every vice have burst wide open, and virtue, as if sickened by the spectacle of human degradation, has almost wholly departed. Providence is continually illustrating the truth, (with which the world should by this time have become familiar,) that our social, civil, and religious state is intimately connected with our views of the sacred, binding character of *the marriage tie.*

The same may be said of the relation existing between parent and child. The wayward youth may escape from parental authority, but he cannot escape from his relationship to those whose blood flows in his veins, nor from the duties which that relationship imposes. The parent may outwardly disown the child, but he can neither dissolve the ties of nature, nor justly ignore their existence.

It also belongs to the nature of the family constitution that it is PERPETUAL. The obligation to right parental influence ceases not with the legal expiration of parental authority. The Bible nowhere bids us remit our kind interest in and care for our offspring, at the age when the law declares them to have become men and women. It is true that they are then supposed to be capable of self-government, but although then passing from under our *rule*, they should still retain a place in our solicitude, our counsels, and our prayers.

There are those who deem themselves absolved from every obligation, natural or moral, towards a member of the family who errs, and hesitate not, in some instances, to debar him the privileges of the home that he has disgraced. Without stopping to discuss the lack of affection displayed by such a course, we simply ask, where, in the word of God, is there any warrant for it? And yet who, but the Creator, can absolve us from a relation which he has himself ordained? Not thus lightly can we shake off our solemn duties, and make another's sin the plea for their evasion. Rather let us throw the more closely about the erring one the sacred influences of the Christian home, which, like a guardian angel, may protect him from the world's temptations, and perchance win him back to duty. So doing, we may ourselves the more hopefully seek the Father's forgiving grace when "overtaken by a fault," and fall confidingly upon the bosom of Him who welcomes the returning prodigal.

We may remark, further, that this relation is perpetual *as a Divine institution in the world.* God has not abrogated it, nor can the voice of man annul it. The lapse of ages has in no way affected it, but, like its twin institution, the Sabbath, it belongs to all time and to every generation. Neither of them shall cease its beneficent office until they end together in the second Paradise; the one being merged into the endless Sabbath, and the other in the united family of the redeemed in glory.

III. Our third topic is the IMPORTANCE of the family constitution.

The best gifts of Providence are generally those that men prize the least. The family, with its delightful influences, like the free air or sunlight, seems to us so much a matter of course that we perhaps fail to realize its value. A little reflection, however, must convince any one that it occupies a high position in God's moral government of the world, and is possessed of the most momentous bearings upon the welfare of the individual, the state, and the race.

This may readily be inferred from the fact that it is *specially ordained by God.* In architecture, the importance of an edifice is generally proportioned to the depth and strength of its foundations. We have seen that the family structure is based upon the appointment of the Creator, as well as upon the most urgent necessities of mankind; and we must therefore regard it as rising to a corresponding height and grandeur of importance.

See, too, what a stress is laid upon its true character and duties in the Scriptures; how it is environed with laws and precepts, and made so much an object of God's jealous care. This signifies the estimation in which our Maker holds it, aud which he would impress upon every mind—just as one's watchfulness in protecting a casket of jewels would naturally be regarded as an indication of its value.

Let there also be borne in mind, *the tremendous power of the family for good or evil.* Who can estimate it? See how characters are moulded, habits formed, and destinies shaped for eternity under its plastic influences. Contemplate the child whose open mind is receiving its first, and therefore lasting, impressions of good or evil. Before him lies a future, that is known only to God. That voice may yet sway unnumbered multitudes of fellow beings; that mind may influence a nation's councils; that soul may, nay it *shall,* thrill through everlasting ages with the bliss of heaven, or suffer endless pangs in torment. We tremble as we try to forecast its destiny, and think of the wonderful possibilities that lie wrapped within it. We instinctively ask, What influences are brought to bear upon this young immortal? We turn to the family in which his lot is cast. Is it a *godless* one? Shall he grow up as one of an irreligious circle, where no voice of prayer is heard, where the name of God is dishonoured and profaned, and holy Sabbath hours are desecrated? Sad lot! Divine grace may indeed yet snatch him from "the burning," but the probabilities are strong that he will fall a victim to surrounding influences—(for how shall the helpless child resist them?) and that whatever power he may hereafter exert in the world will be for evil and not for good, while his prospects for eternity are dark and fearful. Or is he the child of *pious* parents, early dedicated to the Lord, and growing up amid religious influences? Happy lot! for, whatever be his future sphere in life, there is every likelihood that it will be adorned with lovely Christian graces, that he will diffuse around him the charm of godliness, and that endless blessedness awaits him hereafter. Exceptions there may be, and often are, upon both sides, but all will admit that these are, at least, *the probabilities.* Judging from experience and the word of God, are we not warranted in affirming that, had the childhood of Napoleon been nurtured amid the atmosphere of family religion, his manhood might have been that of a Paul; and his career might have blessed, by its sanctified energies, as many as it destroyed? So, too, may we not believe that an Edwards, if subjected in early life to the unhallowed influences of an irreligious home, might have employed his high powers in assailing, instead of fortifying the bulwarks of Christianity? It is true that God is sovereign in the bestowments of his grace, and that there is no converting power in even the most faithful religious training, when viewed by itself; yet there is a heaven-ordained connection between the means and the end, and of all the means that are blessed by the Holy Spirit to men's salvation, none are more influential than those lodged in *the Christian family.*

With what an inconceivable importance, then, is this relation invested! Humble and unnoticed it may be by the world without, but it is the starting point of those lines of influence that shall reach down through all time, and far into the coming eternity. The mother, whose cares and toils may seem narrowed down to a little circle, is perhaps wielding, unconsciously, a power grander than that of any monarch. It may appear to her but a slight thing to clasp tiny hands in prayer, and teach that expanding mind of Christ and heaven; yet few scenes upon earth are more truly sublime, and hers is a task that angels might covet.

Well would it be for us, could we better realize the importance of the family, and the high place that it occupies in the system of the divine government. For then we should hardly dare trifle with its duties, or evade its responsibilities; but, invoking grace from on high to assist us, we should aim at the utmost faithfulness. It is only when we rise to the consideration of its surpassing magnitude, as a powerful means ordained by God to a glorious end, and as a relation whose bearings for good or evil only eternity can measure, that we can duly estimate either the sacredness of its claims, or the value of its privileges.

CHAPTER II.

THE DUTIES AND RESPONSIBILITIES BELONGING TO THE FAMILY RELATION.

Every sphere of influence or action is a divinely ordained sphere of obligation. There are duties pertaining to one's own heart and life, and in close connection with these—or rather, growing out of them as the branches from the tree—are those of the counting-room, the field, the shop, the church, or whatever position the providence of God assigns us. It is therefore but reasonable to infer that *the family* has its appointed duties and responsibilities, which none can evade without defeating, to a greater or less degree, the ends of its institution, and thereby incurring positive guilt.

Upon this subject the word of God is explicit, and we have only to turn to its pages in order to discover the whole of conjugal, parental, and filial duty. He who has instituted the family relation for his own glory, has himself defined the laws that are to govern it, and with such an array of precepts for our guidance as the Scriptures afford, we can easily dispense with those that are of merely human origin.

I. Beginning with the mutual duties of HUSBAND AND WIFE, we find that the one requirement which includes all others, and without which none can be discharged acceptably, is *love*.

"Husbands, love your wives, even as Christ also loved the church, and gave himself for it." "So ought men to love their wives as their own bodies." Eph. v. 25, 28. "Teach the young women to be sober, to love their husbands." Tit. ii. 4. Thus has our Maker clothed with all the sanctions of a religious obligation that affection which affords the only basis of a happy marriage. And what a powerful illustration of the strength of true conjugal love is furnished in the comparison, "even as Christ also loved the church, and gave himself for it!" We cannot conceive of a love more mighty, more unselfish than this, which, we are informed, "passeth knowledge;" yet of this the affection of husband and wife is deemed the most appropriate type. Viewed in such an aspect, it rises above the character of a mere sentiment, and is ennobled into an emblem of the outgoings of the Divine, Infinite heart towards all the redeemed.

The fruits of this affection are as various as are the duties involved in the marriage relation; for those duties are only performed aright, when proceeding from this as their constraining motive. Thus love is ever found to be "the fulfilling of the law." The obligations of sustenance, fidelity, and kind care need hardly be urged upon him who truly loves the partner of his life, neither is it necessary to remind the devoted and affectionate wife of her duty to reverence and cherish her husband. Without pausing, therefore, to dwell upon these minor requirements, let us turn our attention to a class of duties which are more commonly overlooked—namely, those that relate to *the promotion of one another's spiritual well being.*

In the government of God the physical is ever held subordinate to the moral, and the temporal to the eternal. It follows from this that while the rite of marriage has a partial reference to our welfare as social beings, it was chiefly in regard to our moral needs that God said, "It is not good for man to be alone." When the true ends of this relation are fulfilled, it becomes instrumental of such a mutual progress in the Divine life as is rarely attained by any monk or recluse. Then, each strengthens the other's hands and warms the other's heart in their common life-work of glorifying God, and preparing for his service hereafter; and then, indeed, each is "something better than a mere self, by becoming part of a nobler whole."

It is greatly to be regretted that many, from a feeling of false delicacy, or a sense of unwarrantable restraint, fail to make their union thus fruitful of spiritual good. It seems strange that two children of God, who are doubly united by the ties of nature and of grace, while maintaining the closest confidence in regard to temporal matters, and conversing freely upon every other topic of common interest, should yet hold but little communion upon the great themes of religion. The temptation to such a reserve should be strenuously resisted. By the aid of Divine grace it may be wholly overcome, and the way thus opened for loftier attainments and richer enjoyments in the Christian life. The heart is strengthened for duty by the consciousness that another is deeply interested in its struggles; while the thought of the vast influence wielded by the one over the other, and of the corresponding responsibility for the manner in which it is exerted, will quicken to faithfulness, and incite to new spiritual growth. Happy are they who, cemented by the bond of a common union to the Saviour, delight in the interchange of holy thoughts and aspirations, each becoming to the other a "help-meet" indeed for all the toils and trials of the heavenward journey. "Heirs together of the grace of life," they press, hand in hand "towards the mark," and enjoy in their sanctified fellowship sweet foretastes of the blessedness that awaits them hereafter.

But what shall we say of those instances, which, alas! are by no means rare, *in which only one of the parties is a child of God?* The command, "Be ye not unequally yoked together with unbelievers," is not, perhaps, at this day sufficiently obeyed; yet it sometimes occurs that the marriage "yoke" becomes "unequal" by the conversion of the one without the other, long after the formation of this tie. In either case, the Christian so situated is greatly to be commiserated; for what can be more sad than for one to struggle against the adverse influence of ungodliness, when put forth by the partner of his or her life? The upward path, so difficult at the best, becomes doubly arduous when travelled, not merely in solitude, but with a hand that we love pulling us back towards the broad road to death.

The duty of the Christian, under such circumstances, is plain. He must not allow the love of the creature to triumph over that which he owes the Creator, nor permit the dictates of natural affection to overwhelm his convictions of religious duty. This is emphatically set forth in our Saviour's words, "If any man come to me, and hate not"—(that is, in comparison with his love to me)—"his father and mother, and wife, and children, and brethren, and sisters, yea, and his own life also, he cannot be my disciple." Luke xiv. 26. In addition to this negative requirement, there is an imperative obligation to labour for the conversion of the impenitent one. This is clearly inculcated in the Scriptures. Thus Peter writes, "Likewise, ye wives, be in subjection to your own husbands; that if any obey not the word they may also, without the word, *be won by the conversation of the wives;* while they behold your chaste conversation coupled with fear." 1 Pet. iii. 1, 2. The apostle Paul, after exhibiting the duty of the believing husband or wife who may be wedded to an unbeliever, and showing that the bond ought not to be dissolved, inasmuch as the faith of the one parent places the offspring in that relation to God which he styles "holy," (or set apart, included in the covenant,) adds as another reason for maintaining the unequal relation, "For what knowest thou, O wife, whether thou shalt *save thy husband?* or how knowest thou, O man, whether thou shalt *save thy wife?*" 1 Cor. vii. 16.

The dictates of natural affection would seem to coincide strongly with these teachings of the Divine word. If love seeks the best good of its object, how can it, in the instance which we have supposed, do otherwise than aim at that richest of all blessings, salvation, in behalf of one who is destitute of it? To this may be added the thought of the awful responsibility of a Christian who is so situated. We are accountable to God for our every perversion of influence, or neglect of opportunity for doing good. When, therefore, we consider the unbounded influence, and the golden opportunities which the marriage relation involves, who does not see that the degree of responsibility is well nigh immeasurable?

Another motive which should weigh powerfully with the Christian parent may be found in *the influence of an ungodly father or mother upon the minds of children.* It is well known that an evil example is much more likely to be followed than a good one, and that the inclinations of the human heart, from earliest childhood, are more disposed to sin than holiness. Of what avail, then, is the instruction or example of the pious parent, when daily, hourly counteracted by the life of the other who is ungodly? Indeed we must regard the piety of *both parents* as lying at the foundation of religion in the family. But more than this, a neglect of the duty under consideration will always recoil upon the faithless disciple. It is ever the case, that whether holiness put forth its power or not, *sin* is aggressive, and, if not met with counteracting influences, will imperceptibly sap the foundations of piety. Many an one who has hesitated to urge the claims of religion upon an ungodly companion, and who, for the sake of harmony, has compromised his piety, has in after years reaped the bitter fruits of habitual backslidings, or become almost irretrievably entangled in the meshes of worldliness. Others, upon the contrary, more faithful to their trust, have found the flame of their own piety enkindled anew as they laboured for souls that were dear to them, and have experienced the fulfilment of the assurance, "He that watereth shall be watered also himself."

It will, perhaps, be objected that the efforts of the pious wife or husband in this respect are not always attended with success. While this fact cannot justly be regarded as exonerating them from their solemn obligations, we may yet suggest the inquiry whether such efforts are always faithfully and perseveringly exerted? Certain it is that in this, as in other departments of religious duty, God has connected the means with the end, and the general rule holds good, "In due season ye shall reap, if ye faint not." The voice of experience concurs with the word of God in assuring us that patient, continuous prayer and effort are seldom in vain. No doubt the great thing requisite is a stronger *faith* in the prayer, hearing God, and a more unwearying importunity at the mercy-seat.

Two pious women, whose husbands were opposed to religion, agreed to spend one hour daily in prayer for their conversion, which practice they continued for seven years without any visible effect. At length, with hearts full of anguish they met to mingle their griefs, when they resolved that they would persevere till the end of life in the course they had adopted, and that if their husbands *would* go down to destruction, they should go *loaded with their prayers.* Thus they continued for three years longer. About this time one of them was awakened in the night by the mental distress of her husband, who entreated her to pray for him. As soon as the day dawned, she went with an overflowing heart to tell her praying companion that God was about to answer their petitions. Great was her surprise to meet her friend coming upon the same errand. Thus, as the result of their ten years' perseverance in calling mightily upon God, they were permitted to see both their husbands brought upon the same day to realize their undone condition, and at about the same time to accept the Saviour.

Would that there were more of this spirit of persevering prayer in all the churches! For then the sad spectacle, now so common, of the pious wife or husband coming alone to the table of the Lord, and contending, single-handed, against the influences of an impenitent companion over their common offspring, would be less frequently exhibited, while it would be found that many a family, now divided in their spiritual and eternal prospects, would be joined together, husband and wife, brothers and sisters, as partakers in "one Lord, one faith, and one baptism."

II. Of at least equal importance are the duties of the PARENTAL RELATION.

It is an awfully solemn thing to be a parent—to be intrusted with the guardianship of immortal spirits, just entering upon life, whose character and destiny depend to so great a degree upon our faithfulness in duty. What trust can be more precious! What responsibility more vast! Yet, when rightly engaged in, there is no class of duties more fraught with pleasure to the child of God. Few joys are to be compared with those of the faithful parent as, day by day, he watches the unfolding of the tender mind, and impresses upon it those great truths that are capable of making it for ever blessed. And if he rejoices "with trembling," he yet "derives profound satisfaction from the thought, that as he is instrumentally the source of its natural, so he may become that of its spiritual life," and that he is the chosen means through whom that soul, with all its vast capacities, may be added as a rich jewel to the Saviour's crown.

The obligations that this relation involves correspond in magnitude and importance with the parent's high position. Occupying, as he does, a station of commanding influence and authority, like that of a king, or governor, (or perhaps more nearly resembling that of the ancient patriarch,) he is the repository of vast interests, and, in a manner, the arbiter of momentous destinies. Much therefore depends upon his clear understanding of the responsibilities thus devolved upon him. Happily, we need be at no loss upon this subject, for the Divine Founder of the parental relation has given us all the precepts that are requisite in regard to it.

1. The one duty that underlies all others, is *love.* The apostle exhorts mothers to "love their children;" Tit. ii. 4; and if this obligation is not insisted upon in the Scriptures with the frequency and earnestness that characterize some others, it is because it was scarcely deemed necessary thus to enjoin that which is acknowledged by all to be a common dictate of nature. In this respect the parental heart is its own law. It may be taken for granted, that, with those few and rare exceptions which occasionally send a thrill of horror through a community, and which we instinctively brand as *unnatural,* parents do love their offspring. Hard as the flinty rock must be that heart whose affections do

not flow out in a warm, rich current towards the child whom God has given it. There is that in the helplessness, the innocence, the confiding trust of early childhood, which smites the rock of selfishness in the bosom of the misanthrope, and unseals a tide of fond emotion, which otherwise would not have been suspected to exist. All will perceive the wisdom of this provision of our Creator, and its necessary bearing upon the great ends of the family constitution. Without it, the most elaborate code of laws would have been in vain; and that tender care which, however laborious, is still a "labour of love," would have been irksome, if not intolerable; while at the same time, however we might have been constrained by the bare sense of duty to right conduct, our endeavours would have been far less effective, because destitute of this energizing principle.

Assuming, then, the universal existence of this affection, it is obvious that it should habitually *be manifested* to its objects, in ways that are calculated to impress them with a sense of its reality and strength. The heart of childhood is keenly sensitive upon this subject, and depends for much of its happiness upon the consciousness of being beloved. That is a mistaken view of the dignity becoming the head of a family, which regards it as necessary to disguise the fond heart under an aspect of cold authority, and whose constant appeal is rather to the distant reverence than the confiding affection of the child. Those nurtured under such chilling influences may indeed stand in awe of the parent, and be coerced into a sullen obedience; but let it be remembered that it is easier for them afterwards to throw off the weight of authority than the spell of affection, and that all government in which love forms not a part degenerates into despotism, while all reverence that is destitute of this principle becomes simple fear or terror.

Says a writer, "Conversing the other day with an interesting little girl between six and seven years old, I took occasion to impress upon her mind the gratitude due from her to her heavenly Parent, for bestowing upon her so good and kind a father, whom everybody loves. I was perfectly thunderstruck at her answer. Looking me full in the face with her soft blue eyes, she replied, '*He never speaks kind to me.*' Perhaps this Christian parent, harassed with the cares of life, was unconscious that he had roughly checked the fond attentions of his child; but could cares, or the interruptions of his child excuse unkindness or a total want of the tokens of endearment?" It is probable that the larger number of those who err in this respect, do so unconsciously. Oppressed, perhaps, with life's sterner anxieties, the parent thinks not that the hearts of his children are yearning silently for his look of love or kindly caress, and that the endearing word, or answering smile, which would cost him no effort, would thrill their bosoms with joyful satisfaction, and aid incalculably in their discharge of filial duty. Thus God deals with his children, blending with the unapproachable majesty of the Sovereign the grace and love of the fond Father, at all times smiling upon us, and even when he chastens, clasping the recreant child yet closer to his bosom.

It scarcely seems necessary to define the various forms in which parental love may find appropriate expression.

These will readily occur to the judicious mind. It may be remarked, in general, that it will prompt to a deep sympathy in the little pleasures of childhood's heart, and a feeling of commiseration for its griefs. Our heavenly Father assumes the existence of this feeling in the parent's bosom, when he says, "Like as a father *pitieth his children*, so the Lord pitieth them that fear him." There are countless opportunities in the daily experience of every family for such exhibitions of tender consideration. This duty also stands opposed to that hectoring, teasing disposition which sometimes marks the intercourse of parents with their children, and which is denounced in the Apostle's exhortation, "Fathers, provoke not your children to anger, lest they be discouraged." An unreasonable rebuke, or impatient word or frown, or a chastisement for which there is no real occasion, may deeply wound the heart that is aiming at sincere obedience, and may, if often repeated, crush those tendrils of affection that were twining lovingly about us, and which it should ever be our aim to foster and develop. At the same time, however, let care be exercised that this love do not retard, instead of promoting the great purposes of family training. For instance, that is a weak overweening fondness, and one indeed that defeats itself, which feels constrained to gratify every caprice of the childish mind. The same may be said of that which substitutes mere flattery for judicious approbation, or which visibly attaches to the person rather than the character, or to the beautiful body rather than the priceless soul. That is the purest, holiest affection which is ever held subservient to duty, and which is willing to sacrifice the present gratification of its object to his greater good hereafter.

Upon the exercise and intelligent exhibition of parental love, depends, under God, much of our success in all the duties that this relation involves. It is to the family what oil is to the machine ; lubricating every wheel of influence or of action, and causing that to move in easy, silent harmony, which otherwise must jar and conflict. It is a spell whose sweet influence disarms rebellion, conquers passion, opens the heart to lessons of wisdom, and thus wins it to paths of pleasantness and peace. Let its atmosphere pervade the home, and it becomes a type of heaven, where the Divine Father sways with the sceptre of his love the hearts of all saints and angels.

2. Another important duty of parents is that of solemnly *consecrating their children to God.* This was enjoined upon the Old Testament Church in the ordinance of circumcision, which was the prescribed method of dedication to Jehovah, and the seal of the Abrahamic covenant, and which was to be administered to the child when he was but eight days old. Its place is now occupied by the Christian rite of Baptism, which, being significant of the same great truths, and the seal of the same covenant, is equally obligatory upon the pious parent.

The reasonableness of this requirement flows necessarily from the fact that all that we possess is the Lord's. Whatever be the offering that we render him, whether of strength, talents, riches, or our very souls, we may well say of them as David did in regard to the gifts towards building the temple, "All things come of thee, and of thine own have we given thee." The same is eminently true of our offspring; and if we are required to dedicate to him of our worldly abundance, how much stronger is the obligation to surrender to him those intelligent, living, active beings, who are so adapted by their nature and the design of their creation to glorify God! If, in the spirit of pious consecration, that is to mark the church's latter day glory, "Holiness to the Lord" shall be written upon even the utensils of God's house, and the very bells of the horses, surely it should be inscribed by fond parental faith and prayer upon the minds that are budding into immortality, and the hearts that are expanding to the embrace of an endless destiny.

Let it also be borne in mind that these rich treasures are only given us *in trust*, and therefore are to be improved to the Divine glory. Think not, fond parent, that the little ones who cluster about you, and whose confiding love sweetens so many hours of life, are merely sent to confer pleasure upon you! They are a sacred charge entrusted for a season to your guardianship, to be trained by you for the heavenly kingdom. Christ says of them, "Feed *my lambs*," plainly implying that they are *his*, and are ours only to feed and nourish for the good Shepherd, being loaned to us for a season for our good and theirs; and when we sometimes forget this fact, and selfishly deem them all our own, does not the Shepherd's voice thrill us with the whisper, "These are *my* lambs," as he plucks one and another from our sight, and transfers them to the fold above? We may not then keep back these best gifts of God, nor regard them as exclusively our own.

"These are my jewels," said Cornelia, the mother of

the Gracchi, pointing to her children. May we not imagine the Saviour, as he turns his dying eye upon us, pointing with the hand that was pierced for our transgressions to our children, and saying, "Give me your jewels in slight return for this loving sacrifice, that I may set them in my heavenly diadem, where they shall sparkle, undimmed, for ever!" And what is the response of the pious heart? Shall we refuse the Lord that bought us, and say, "We will surrender all besides to thee, but leave us these?" Let us rather exclaim, "Accept them, Lord, as our best gifts—our heart treasures! Let the casket of thy love enclose them, for there only are they secure!" Let every Christian parent adopt from the heart, in reference to each and every child whom God has given him, the words of the pious Hannah, "I have lent him to the Lord; as long as he liveth, he shall be lent to the Lord."

As an important motive to this duty, we may add the delightful fact that all children of believers *are included in God's covenant with his people.* The Divine promise made to Abraham, and which, let it be remembered, lay at the foundation of God's visible church, was to him *and his seed after him* in their generations. The engagements into which God then entered with his people have never been abrogated, and the great body of the church in all ages have recognized the privilege of their children as included in his covenant with themselves. Believers are said by Isaiah to be "the seed of the blessed of the Lord, and their offspring with them." "The promise," said Peter, "is to you and your children."

Now what should be the effect of this glorious doctrine? It evidently ought to impel us, first of all, to *the private dedication of our children to their covenant God.* Upon bended knees, under a strong realization of the solemnity of the act, and in the exercise of a firm faith in the promise, we should surrender them to God, recognizing his title to them, pleading his known interest in them, and claiming for them the blessing of his covenanted grace.

Having done this, the *public* act of consecration follows, in the use of the ordinance of *baptism.* This is not the place for an extended discussion of the question, whether infants ought to be baptized—yet as there is a too prevalent neglect of this duty in Christian families, and as many entertain erroneous views as to its nature and importance, we shall briefly present the chief arguments upon which this doctrine is founded.

In the seventeenth chapter of the book of Genesis, we read that God entered into a covenant with Abraham in which he declared, "I will establish my covenant between me and thee, and thy seed after thee, in their generations, for an everlasting covenant, to be a God unto thee and to thy seed after thee." Gen. xvii. 7. This covenant includes in its ample scope, not only the lineal descendants of the patriarch, but the whole visible church—all professed believers. "They which are of the faith," writes Paul to the Gentiles, "the same are the children of Abraham." Gal. iii. 7. "If ye are Christ's, then are ye Abraham's seed, and heirs according to the promise." Gal. iii. 29. This covenant also embraces in its provisions *both old and young,* parents and children. In confirmation of this, God immediately

4*

ratified his covenant by instituting the ordinance of circumcision, and directing its application to infants of eight days old.

Here, then, at the very first organization of the church—(for although there were believers in the world previous to this transaction, there were none of the characteristics of a visible, organized church)—we find *infants* admitted, by a sealing ordinance, to its membership. We here find God binding himself in a covenant relation with Abraham and his seed after him, or his children, and therefore with all the members of his church and their seed—with every circumcised Jew and his offspring, and, as the church is always one and the same, with every Christian believer and his offspring, through all generations. Now it will be seen that the admission of infants to the church by the appropriate rite was as much a part of the covenant as was the promise that it sealed; and that to do away with the one would be to abolish the other. If, therefore, the covenant is still in force, "I will be a God to thee and to thy seed after thee," then the conclusion is irresistible, that our seed are to be initiated, by the appropriate rite of the Christian dispensation, into the visible church, and to receive the seal of their covenant relation to God.

That this covenant is still in force is evident from the fact that the Scriptures nowhere give the remotest hint of its having been abrogated. It did not expire with the ceremonial law, for that was not promulgated until long after this was established; and was only added to serve a temporary purpose, having fulfilled which, it vanished. Besides, there is *no new covenant,* and if we have not this to rest upon as the ground of our relation to God, then we have not any; a conclusion of itself sufficient to establish its perpetuity. It follows from this that the law of infant church membership is to this day unrepealed, that the initiatory ordinance is still to be applied to the seed of believers, and therefore that baptism, the rite of the new dispensation which answers to circumcision in the old, and which immediately followed its abrogation, is to be administered to them. In the absence of any scriptural proof that God has ever annulled the ancient constitution of his church or forbidden us those privileges which were granted his people until the coming of Christ, the conclusion is unavoidable that *infants of believers are to be baptized.*

If, then, this is an ordinance of the church, *it is imperatively binding upon all who are its members.* The obligation of the ancient Jew to circumcise his child, was no greater than is that of every Christian parent to dedicate him to God in baptism. Indeed, how can he plead the Divine promise in regard to his offspring, who by neglecting this duty becomes himself a covenant-breaker with Jehovah? Upon the other hand, with what confidence may the faithful parent claim the fulfilment of those engagements by which God has bound himself to him and his seed after him! Having obediently placed his children within the pale of the visible church, he may the more hopefully pray and labour that they may also be inclosed in the inner, spiritual fold of Christ. For, let none suppose that their position as heirs of the covenant of promise will, in itself, convert and save them. No; it rather obliges us to the use of those means by which they may be made partakers of the covenanted grace. It is a woful perversion of precious truth to evade responsibility upon the plea of the Divine promise. Its true and reasonable effect will be to incite us to more earnest diligence in our children's behalf, for it assures us that they are the Lord's, that to him they are solemnly consecrated, and for him they are to be trained and nurtured.

Among the many advantages, near and remote, of a discharge of this duty may be placed that of *its moral influence upon the minds of the persons baptized.* The infant may be unconscious of the import of the sacred rite, but in after years it becomes an argument for devotion to God's service, with which no parent or child can afford to dispense. The thought that solemn vows have been pronounced over him in the sanctuary, binding him to the Lord—vows sealed by the symbol of atoning blood, and for whose fulfilment he is himself become responsible, is one that may well weigh upon the mind and heart of the youth, and incite him to duty. The question with him is, and it must often obtrude upon his hours of serious reflection, "not whether he shall contract or avoid an allegiance which has hitherto had no claims upon him; but whether he shall acknowledge or *renounce* an allegiance under which he drew his first breath? Whether he shall disown the Prince of life, and waive his interest in his church? Whether he shall disclaim the God of his fathers, forswear his consecration to his service? Not whether he shall be a simple unbeliever, but whether he shall display his unbelief in the form of *apostasy?* That is the question, and an awful one it is!"*

The mere *act* of consecration, however, does not fulfil the parents' whole duty in this respect. This is to be followed up by *an habitual regarding of his offspring as belonging to the Lord.* Consistency would seem to require that, having dedicated them to him, all our subsequent treatment of them be in strict accordance with that fact. It should colour all our intercourse, point our instructions, and direct our plans and purposes in regard to them. When tempted to sacrifice their higher interests to temporal aggrandizement, or to indulge in those selfish dreams of the future which excessive fondness may suggest, let the thought, "they are the Lord's," recall us to duty and nerve us for its discharge.

Among the papers of the mother of the devoted missionary Samuel J. Mills, was recently brought to light a fragment of an unfinished letter, intended as a reply to her son's announcement of his decision to go upon a foreign mission. It dwelt pathetically upon the trial of parting with him, and the dangers to which he would be exposed. She had proceeded but a little way in this strain, however, when the thought that she had given her son to the Lord overcame the dictates of selfish affection. Throwing aside what she had written, she began another letter in another strain, and told her son *to go.* The fragment alluded to remains a monument of her struggle and her triumph.

Much is also to be gained by *impressing upon the*

---

* Dr. Mason.

minds of the young that they are thus set apart to the Master's service in whatever sphere he may assign to them, and that, like the holy vessels of the ancient temple, they cannot be withdrawn from that service without the crime of sacrilege. It will be found that this habitual recognition of the truth we are considering will aid materially in the task of rearing them for God, and will give a healthful impulse to right parental effort. And what a plea is this to present at the throne of grace, "they are the Lord's!" In all their devious wanderings we may say,

"Remember still that they are thine,
That thy dear, sacred name they bear!
Think that the seal of love divine,
The sign of covenant grace they wear!"

This thought will also go far towards inspiring us with quiet resignation, when God is pleased to transfer them to his higher and more glorious service. However we might be disposed to repine at losing *our own* dear offspring, the thought that they are the Lord's by a stronger tie than they are ours, being his *property*, while they are ours only as a temporary *loan*, to be recalled at the Divine pleasure, is calculated to promote a sweet submission as we say, "The Lord gave, and the Lord hath taken away; blessed be the name of the Lord."

CHAPTER III.

PARENTAL DUTIES AND RESPONSIBILITES, CONTINUED.

3. A THIRD duty of parents to their children is that of *government and discipline.*

This is frequently enjoined in the word of God. "He that spareth his rod hateth his son: but he that loveth him chasteneth him betimes." Prov. xiii. 24. "Foolishness is bound up in the heart of a child, but the rod of correction shall drive it far from him." Prov. xxii. 15. "Correct thy son and he shall give thee rest; yea, he shall give delight unto thy soul." Prov. xxix. 17.

These precepts, and other similar ones with which the Scriptures abound, are founded in wisdom and beneficence, and are adapted to the whole character of the family constitution. The position of the parent, as set forth by Him who has ordained it, is one of authority, while that of the child is one of subjection. This authority is delegated by God, and is to be employed in fulfilment of his will, and with a view to his glory. The child, with all his endearing attractions, is still the possessor of a depraved nature, and evinces his relationship to the first transgressor by exhibiting a perverse independence of will and impatience under wholesome restraint. If the well ordered family resembles Eden in its pure pleasures, so, like it, it is not without its wise prohibitions; and the first impulse of childhood is to taste the forbidden fruit.

For this reason the first step of the parent may well be *to establish his authority*, and form the tender mind to habits of obedience. Until this be done, every other effort will be comparatively in vain. The wisest counsels are apt to fall unheeded upon one who recognizes no other law than his own will; while he who is accustomed to obey is not only a most hopeful subject of parental instruction, but is the better prepared for the service of the heavenly Father. And in speaking of authority, we use the term in its strict, absolute sense. Were the child introduced into the world with full grown powers of mind, and the keen moral perceptions of the matured and cultivated heart, it would perhaps be proper always to reason with it, and to substitute argument and persuasion for simple command. It will, however, be seen, that under such circumstances there would be no occasion for parental influence. The truth is, the mental and moral faculties of childhood are *to be developed* by the parent, and it is as a means to such development that his authority is to be exercised. We are often obliged to give and enforce commands, the reasons of which are above the comprehension of children; and even should they appreciate them in their full force, they may still be disposed to follow the bent of their inclinations. We should indeed recognize their character as intelligent beings, by generally assigning the motives of our conduct, and enjoining nothing that is unreasonable; yet they should be taught to obey, not merely the voice of argument, but that of authority, and to regard the parents' *will* as the law of the household.

This, so far from conflicting with that mutual love which lies at the foundation of parental and filial duty, is the rather its appropriate fruit. For he who seeks the best good of his offspring will endeavour so to govern them, that the dictates of his affection may be the most effectively carried out; and the child who best loves his parents, and the most confides in their wisdom, will ever be the most ready to submit to their authority.

Upon this subject, two extremes are to be carefully avoided. Some err by an *excessive leniency*. To so great an extent is this carried at the present day as to have given rise to the sarcastic remark, "It is said that there is less family government now than formerly. It is a mistake. There is as much government as ever, with this difference; the parents formerly governed the children, but now the children govern the parents." That is a mistaken policy which sacrifices the future good of the child to his present indulgence. It may be pleasant to avoid the struggle with self-will, and the effort of subduing it, but will it be as agreeable in coming years to reap the fruits of such neglect in the sad ruin of a son or daughter? Painful as it may be to harrow the young heart with the grief of chastisement, may it not, thereby, like the harrowed field, be the better prepared for the "good seed?"

The experience of the world in this respect has amply verified the proverb, "He that spareth his rod, hateth his son." "My father was too easy with me," exclaimed a young man in college, upon being remonstrated with for the sin of intemperance. He admitted that he was doing wrong, that he was on the road to ruin; and on being told that he was not compelled to drink, he answered, "No, not compelled; but you do not know what it is to get a taste for liquor. I am a miserable fellow; *my father was too easy with me when I was a boy.*" "He was expelled from college, and died a few years after. If any change took place in his habits, it was not known to the narrator."

A most striking case in point is afforded in the history of Aaron Burr. As the eldest son of President Edwards was congratulating a friend upon having a fine family of sons, he said to him with much earnestness, "Remember, there is but one mode of family government. I have brought up and educated fourteen boys, two of whom I brought up or rather suffered to grow up, without the rod. One of these was my youngest brother; and the other *Aaron Burr,* my sister's only son—" (both of whom had lost their parents in infancy)—"and from both my observation and experience, I tell you, sir, 'maple sugar government' will never answer. Beware how you let the first act of disobedience in your little boys go unnoticed, and, unless evidence of repentance be manifest, unpunished." What an awful lesson! The unrestrained youth above alluded to, became the vile, dissolute, unprincipled man, described by one as "a hater of all mankind, a trifler with all woman-kind, violating all the rules of hospitality in the license of his behaviour; an infidel, a blasphemer, and a murderer, cursing the world to the age of fourscore." Comment is needless.

Another extreme against which the faithful parent will equally guard, is that of *undue severity*. His authority is not magisterial, but parental, and its chief appeal ought therefore to be not to fear, but to love. Where government and discipline are seasonably commenced and rightly administered, there will rarely be occasion for severe measures. When these are rendered necessary, it should be shown that they are dictated rather by affection than anger. As was aptly said by Sir Walter Raleigh, "A man must first govern himself, ere he be fit to govern a family." The too frequent use of the rod, or the resorting to those methods of ingenious *torture* which form with some the chief staple of family government, tend rather to harden than soften the young and tender heart, and by awakening a sense of injustice, to weaken parental authority. We need not resort to the rod when a word or a look may suffice, and should enforce obedience not so much by the severity as the certainty of punishment. We should beware of too strongly exciting the fears of children. Most frightful consequences have sometimes ensued from thoughtless appeals to this principle. Says an English writer, "I knew, in Philadelphia, as fine, and sprightly, and intelligent a child as ever was born, made an idiot for life, by being, when about three years old, shut into a dark closet, by a maid servant, in order to terrify it into silence." A wholesome, kind, and judicious discipline will be found sufficient for every emergency, and being once firmly established, will become the basis upon which to rear the throne of love, and will prepare the way for affection to exert its constraining power, and bring its subjects beneath its sway.

It is also important to an intelligent family government, that the parent consider *the wide difference that exists in the dispositions of children.* A course of procedure that would be required in the case of a wilful, headstrong child, might be highly injurious when brought to bear upon one who is mild, timid, and sensitive. A naturally good disposition may be spoiled by mismanagement, and a bad one greatly improved by right training.

Besides the incidental benefits that accrue from a faithful discharge of this duty, and they are many, it will be found materially to promote the great end of the family, which must ever be kept in view, the training of young minds and hearts to the service and glory of God. As the essence of sin consists in the opposing of our wills to that of God, so it is the chief aim of religion to subdue our wills, and bring them into subjection to the Divine; and what a grand preparative for this is afforded in the Christian home! The child who has learned the lesson of unquestioning obedience is thereby the better prepared to bow before the will of God. Accustomed from earliest infancy to "the obedience of faith," there is that within him which responds the more readily to the claims of his Maker, when he begins clearly to apprehend them. Mrs. Wesley, the mother of the celebrated divine, speaking in a letter of the management of children, says, "I insist upon conquering *the will* of children betimes, because this is the only strong and rational foundation of a religious education, without which both precept and example will be ineffectual. But when this is thoroughly done, then a child is capable of being governed by the reason and piety of its parents, till its own understanding comes to maturity, and the principles of religion have taken root in the mind."

4. Another important duty of the parent is *Instruction.* This is strongly set forth in the commands of God to his ancient people. Next in importance to their obligation to heed and obey the Divine teachings was that of transmitting them to their children. "Teach them thy sons and thy sons' sons." "And ye shall teach them your children, speaking of them when thou sittest in thine house, and when thou walkest by the way, when thou liest down, and when thou risest up." Deut. iv. 9; xi. 19. To the same effect are the precepts of the New Testament: "Ye fathers, provoke not your children to wrath; but bring them up in the nurture and admonition of the Lord." Eph. vi. 4.

God has thus appointed the parent to be the chief educator of the child, and has made the home the scene where, most of all, he is to be schooled in Divine truth, and trained for his service. The genial influences of the family circle, with its endearing sympathies and associations, and its glad flow of filial love and trust, make it preëminently the spot where the lambs of the flock are to be fed and nourished unto everlasting life. It should be no stranger's voice that instils the first rudiments of truth into the infant mind; and no parent, who values his or her privileges aright, will leave to others this blessed task. For, not only do the simple lessons of Divine truth possess an added interest and power when falling from the lips of a fond parent, but who would not desire that the earliest associations of their child in religious things should be linked in with the loved tones of a father's or mother's voice? It is said that Constantine the Great, though he appointed men of the most approved piety to be the teachers of his children, "was himself their instructor in Divine things, to lead them to immortal blessedness."

It is to be feared that the multiplied facilities for religious instruction which exist at the present day have caused many to lose sight of this important duty, and to shift upon others the burden of their responsibility. But we have no right to delegate this solemn trust. The obligation to the *home instruction* of their children is laid upon every parent in the words, "*Ye* shall teach them your children, speaking of them *when thou sittest in thine house.*" There are some who look upon the Sabbath-school as a substitute for the good old practice of our fathers in this respect. Never was there a greater mistake. It is indeed a beneficent institution, and a valuable *auxiliary* to fireside education, but it was never intended to supplant it. Let our children derive from it all the benefit they can, but let the parent also see to it that they receive at home, under his own eye and from his own lips, thorough, systematic instruction in Divine truth.

Would that in all Christian families might be witnessed the spectacle which in past generations has characterized the households of faith, and which is still frequently met with, of the whole family gathered upon a Sabbath evening in a pleasant circle, repeating their lessons from the Bible and Catechism, and holding delightful converse upon the grand themes of redemption! Now an infant voice lisps forth a little hymn; then others recite their verses, or narrate some "sweet story of old" gathered from pages of Scripture—the parents interspersing the exercises with necessary comments, or appropriate words of kind counsel; then the song of praise ascends from the little circle, whose mingled voices symbolize their glad union of hearts; and then the fervent prayer. Upon such a scene, we may well believe, the angels gaze with delighted interest, while the Father smiles on it approvingly. Happy is the home that is enriched with such associations. Happy the child or man whose earliest memories are linked in with such hallowed hours. They cannot be forgotten, and often they arrest the wanderer, and are made the means of bringing him back to his Father's house.

The proper *themes* of parental instruction are sufficiently indicated in the precepts already quoted. While not neglecting those lesser branches of education that lie at the foundation of all mental and moral culture, let the chief stress be laid upon informing the mind and heart in Divine truth. The intellectual ought ever to be held subordinate to the spiritual; and he who would not destroy the intended balance of the mental and moral faculties will be careful how he forces the brain at the expense of the heart, or makes mere literary attainment an end, instead of a simple means to an end higher than itself. Let the mind be cultivated, for it is a glorious part of our nature, and one for whose improvement or neglect we are justly accountable to our Creator; yet let its culture be made tributary to that highest wisdom, the glorifying of God, and preparation for eternity. The duty is devolved upon the parent of answering wisely those great questions, which sometimes will obtrude even upon childhood's mind—"For what purpose do I live? What are my relations to my Maker, and what is my destiny?"

It follows from this that *the Bible* should be the principal text book in the family. And here we cannot but recur to the wonderful adaptedness of God's word to the minds of the young. "It is too simple, too childish in some of its parts," says the infidel, "to have emanated from the Infinite mind, and to bind the faith of cultivated intellects." But God is wiser than man, "and God hath chosen the weak things of the world to confound the things which are mighty." Knowing as we do the power of early impressions, must we not conclude that if religion is to prevail among men, it must make its appeal to the young, and that its truths must be among the first that address the mind of childhood? It is therefore to be expected that a revelation from God to man will be more or less adapted to the tender mind, and that while containing logical and didactic statements for the mature intellect, or the "strong meat" of doctrine, it will not be destitute of its "milk for babes." It is, then, no slight evidence of the wisdom of the great Revealer, that his word abounds in those simple narratives, and beautiful parables which so interest the little child, and instruct it, in an attractive manner, in the duties and rewards of piety. The stories of Moses, and Samuel, and Josiah, and the charming account of "the child Jesus," have perhaps exerted as powerful an influence for good as the matchless arguments of the apostle Paul. The simplicity of the Bible, therefore, and its appropriateness to those whose ignorance or extreme youth ill qualifies them for processes of abstruse reasoning, affords as strong a plea for its inspiration as does the opposite fact, that it contains "things hard to be understood."

In this peculiarity of the Scriptures may be found strong presumptive evidence of the duty we are now considering. God has placed the Bible in our hands as his own appointed means of instructing our offspring, and it is to be employed accordingly;—the parent drawing from it as from a full store-house, judiciously selecting those narratives that will interest and attract, and by means of them illustrating the truths of religion. By so doing, the Bible becomes clothed with the most powerful charms in their estimation, and ever remains associated in their minds with delightful reminiscences of childhood. Let them not, however, be taught to regard it as a mere *story book*, but be made to commit to memory many of its precepts, especially those that fell from the Saviour's lips. They should also be taught to reverence its authority as the very word of God, and in the exercise of that trust which is far more natural than doubt to the little child, to confide implicitly in its teachings.

The following extract from Coleman's "Ancient Christianity Exemplified," exhibits the practice of the primitive Christians in this respect. "The tender solicitude of these early Christians for the religious instruction of their children is one of their most beautiful characteristics. They taught them even at the earliest dawn of intelligence the sacred names of God and the Saviour. They sought to lead the infant minds of their children up to God, by familiar narratives from Scripture, of Joseph, of young Samuel, of Josiah and of the holy child Jesus. The history of the patriarchs and prophets, apostles and holy men, whose lives are narrated in the sacred volume, were the nursery tales with which they sought to form the tender minds of their children. As the mind of the child expanded, the parents made it their sacred duty and delightful task daily to exercise him in the recital of select passages of Scripture relating to the doctrines and duties of religion. The Bible was the entertainment of the fireside. It was the first, the last, the only school book almost, of the child; and sacred psalmody the only song with which his infant cry was hushed as he was lulled to rest on his mother's arm."

In connection with the Bible, *the Catechism* may profitably be employed as affording a connected and systematic view of its doctrines. It is sometimes objected that young children are incapable of fully comprehending the brief, terse statements of truth which these helps contain. While endeavouring as far as possible to obviate this difficulty by proper explanations, let it at the same time be remembered that much is gained by impressing the mind even with "the *form* of sound words;" and that in after years the doctrines thus inculcated may be, and indeed often are, recalled, with a great power for good. History has proved that the church has been the most free from the inroads of error when most closely adhering to catechetical instruction; and it cannot be doubted that of those families which unhappily become divided in faith and doctrine, the greater part are reared in the neglect of this means of grace.

As is the case with every duty, so with this, *much depends upon the manner in which it is discharged.* There is such a thing as making instruction irksome and repulsive, and thus defeating its true end. Some persons grow up with a dislike to the Bible and all religious truth, which may be partially attributed to the circumstance of its being associated in their minds with long, weary hours of childhood's study, or with its burdensome tasks, and even punishments. Let us deal with children as they are, imaginative, emotional creatures, easily interested in a narrative, but apt to be repelled by bare, lengthy statements of doctrine; and while aiming sedulously at a thorough, systematic course of training, our task will be greatly facilitated by the use of illustrations drawn from familiar objects around them. While insisting upon their receiving lessons of heavenly wisdom, let the truth be impressed by every possible means that "her ways are ways of pleasantness, and all her paths are peace."

Parental duty, however, is not fulfilled by the mere instructions of the lip or book. Of equal importance with these is the voice of *example.* The imitative powers of childhood are too well known to require remark. The infant tries to copy the very gestures and movements of the parent, and in regard to the young it holds preëminently true that "actions speak louder than words." This is a kind of education that is carried on by every parent, whether he will or not. However he may neglect verbal instruction, he cannot help teaching by his daily life, nor prevent the predominant features of that life from reproducing themselves in his offspring. And it is generally the case that if the example and precept materially differ, the triumph will be upon the side of the former; while if both concur in instilling right principles, they possess a united force that is well nigh irresistible. It is related of a young man who was about to be ordained to the gospel ministry, that he declared himself to have once been nearly betrayed into infidelity, "but," he added, "there was one argument in favour of Christianity which I could never refute—*the consistent conduct of my own father.*"

It is scarcely to be wondered at that the gay and frivolous parent, whose whole career is marked by worldliness and folly, finds it difficult to lead his children in paths of piety; for how can they be expected to regard as a necessity that which they see daily ignored and neglected before their eyes? They who would cultivate religion in the family must assign it its true position in their own hearts and lives, and thereby not only point to heaven, but "lead the way." The most faithful and long continued instructions of the lip may in an instant be neutralized by an act that is in opposition to them. A well merited reproof upon this subject was once conveyed by Dr. Dwight, President of Yale College, who was himself a monument to parental faithfulness. A gentleman who was calling upon him was so annoyed by a little boy of the doctor's, that he told him he would give him a dollar if he would keep still while he talked with his father. The boy instantly became quiet. When the gentleman had finished his call, he was about to depart without paying the boy; whereupon Dr. Dwight put a dollar into his hand, saying, "You promised my boy a dollar for good behaviour. Give him that as you promised. If, *sir, we lie, our children will be liars also.*"

5. The most important duty of all, and the one to which every other should be held subservient, is that of *seeking the conversion of our children.*

This obligation is implied in all those precepts which inculcate the duty of religious instruction. We have not fulfilled the Divine purpose in the education of our offspring, when we have informed their minds in Divine truth. We are not to rest satisfied until we can discern its workings upon their hearts, and its issue in their lives. A theoretical acquaintance with the scheme of redemption will not, of itself, save the soul. No truth is so thoroughly practical in its aims and bearings as Bible truth, and none can be said truly to understand it, who know it not experimentally. The chief end of religious family training is declared in the words of Moses, after rehearsing the duties of the people: "Set your hearts unto all the words which I testify among you this day, which ye shall *command your children to observe to do, all the words of this law.*" Deut. xxxii. 46. That parental government, in its true idea, has reference to the piety of the children, is evident from God's commendation of Abraham, "For I know him that he will command his children and his household after him, *and they shall keep the way of the Lord.*" Gen. xviii. 19.

Religion, then, should not be presented to the view of our children as a mere system of belief, to be simply understood and assented to, but as a practical, living reality;—each being made to feel that he has *a soul to save;* and all the persuasive powers of the parent being exerted in impressing from earliest childhood this great truth. To aim at any thing less than their personal piety is to defeat the very purpose of the family constitution, to pervert its means and appliances, and to abuse a solemn trust. The parent may secure the temporal and social well being of his offspring, may train them for stations of honour and affluence, and even for a high degree of usefulness in the world; yet if, with all this, he has not faithfully laboured for the *salvation of their souls*, he is guilty of the veriest trifling. He has sacrificed what God designed to be the main purpose of their lives to ends that are merely incidental; and if they perish, may not some portion of their blood be found upon his skirts?

A parent who once continued for several days in a state of beastly drunkenness, only came to his senses to find that his helpless child had starved to death. It will be admitted that the execrations of the outraged community in which this occurred, could hardly have been too severe. Another parent intoxicated, not in body but in mind, with the ardour of money making, or the allurements of fashionable pleasure, recovers from his giddy, *lifelong* oblivion, to find that his children are perishing by the horrid "second death," for the lack of those influences which God had made it his duty to exert. Now which of these is the worse? Which is the most criminal in the sight of God? and whose neglect is attended with the most disastrous consequences?

It is difficult to realize the awful responsibility of the parent in this respect, or precisely to define its limits.

When we have to do with imperishable souls, whose value is so great that, in the estimation of Him who best knows their worth, "the whole world" is no compensation for the loss of one of them, we may well confess ourselves unable to calculate the interests involved in the question of their salvation or damnation. Yet we may at least conclude that none can trifle with so precious a trust without incurring aggravated guilt. The thought that we are in any way accountable to God for the endless destiny that awaits our offspring, would seem to be enough to humble every parent in the dust, and to incite him to the utmost fidelity. That we are thus accountable is implied in the whole nature of the family institution, and is set forth in the teachings of the word of God. If it is true that the sins of parents are visited upon their children, it is also the case that the children's sins, when resulting from the unfaithfulness of those who should have trained them up aright, are sometimes visited upon the parents. Witness the Divine curse pronounced upon Eli, "because his sons made themselves vile, and he restrained them not:" "Therefore," said God, "have I sworn unto the house of Eli that the iniquity of Eli's house shall not be purged with sacrifice or offering for ever." 1 Sam. iii. 13, 14.

But upon this subject, we may appeal to the dictates of *natural affection*. What Christian parent who loves his child can do otherwise than seek his conversion to God? Whatever may be the views of the ungodly upon this point, the believer in the Scriptures well knows that no blessing is to be compared with this, and that he who dies without it, might better never have been born. He therefore has no true appreciation of the religion that he professes, who had rather see his son a Napoleon than a Judson, or a Crœsus or Girard, rather than a Harlan Page. And who can contemplate without a shudder the thought that the young life which we nourish and support shall employ its strength in opposition to the Creator, and the soul which we are daily, hourly impressing for good or evil, wail for ever in torment? Upon the other hand, what thought so delightful as that of becoming the means of spiritual life and blessedness to these objects of our hearts' affections? Of all the joys connected with the family relation, this surely is the loftiest, that our efforts may be blessed to the securing of an "eternal weight of glory" to those we so tenderly love.

Then to this end let the parent devote his best energies. Surely it is well worthy of all the toil that can be brought to bear upon it. It is indeed true that human effort is unavailing, unless it be attended with the Holy Spirit's influences; yet many are the promises to parental faithfulness, and experience proves that it is seldom, if ever, in vain. It is also true that our best endeavours in this, as in other respects, will fall far short of our whole duty; yet God mercifully accepts our imperfect obedience, and is ever ready to assist those who honestly attempt to discharge their solemn trust. He "keepeth covenant for ever." He hath said, "I will pour my Spirit upon thy seed, and my blessing upon thine offspring."

The consideration of the means best adapted to promote so desirable an object, as well as of other parental duties bearing upon the end of family religion, will more appropriately claim attention in a subsequent chapter.

CHAPTER IV.

THE DUTIES OF CHILDREN TO THEIR PARENTS.

III. A THIRD class of duties pertaining to the family, are THOSE OF CHILDREN TO THEIR PARENTS.

1. It seems scarcely necessary to insist at length upon so self-evident a duty as that of *filial love.* It would appear as if there were no virtue which could be more safely assumed as universally existing, than this. It would be strange indeed if the child, nurtured from infancy by affection's hand, and instrumentally indebted for all his joys and comforts to the patient, self-sacrificing devotion of fond parents, could cherish any other emotion towards them. Yet as the natural heart is "enmity against God," it is no cause for surprise that it is sometimes the same in regard to the earthly parent, whose claims upon its affection and gratitude are so much less than those of the Divine. Instances there are of filial hate and ingratitude which may well bring a blush to the cheek of humanity, and cause us to mourn and confess the depravity in which it originates. A few thoughts, therefore, upon this subject will not be deemed inappropriate.

This is one of those obligations that are so deeply engraven by the finger of God upon our hearts, that they needed not to be urged with frequency in the written word. We may, however, regard it as included in the import of the fifth commandment, "Thou shalt honour thy father and thy mother, that thy days may be long upon the land which the Lord thy God giveth thee;" for love is the basis of true reverence, whether exercised towards God or man, and that is but the semblance of honour, which is destitute of this principle. The same may be said of every filial duty. None of them can be discharged with acceptance to God, or ease and profit to ourselves, unless their foundation be laid broad and deep in the heart's warm affections. The human family is in this respect a mirror of the Divine. No truth in religion is more plain than that our obedience to God must flow rather from love than from fear. "If a man love me, he will keep my words." "He that loveth me not keepeth not my sayings." And here we have a powerful motive to parental affection; for if "like begets like," the one who exercises and displays it is not only the better qualified thereby to fulfil his own obligations, but is fostering in the bosoms of his offspring that which will tend to render them the more dutiful and obedient.

The bearings of this principle upon religion in the family are very evident. While greatly promoting a successful moral training, by inspiring confidence in and obedience to parental instruction, it also prepares the heart, in some degree, for the love of its heavenly Parent. Experience proves that those who are destitute of natural affection are the least likely of any to love God; while the affectionate child is, other things being equal, a more hopeful subject of renewing grace. In that frequent figure by which God compares his love to his people to that of the earthly parent, is also included the corresponding truth that our love to him resembles the filial affection of the child. So that this obligation is not intended to stop short with its immediate fulfilment, but, in the wise economy of grace, is designed as a preparative for higher duties, and for the fervid outgoing of all the heart, and mind, and soul, and strength to our Creator. Thus may the instinctive fondness of the infant, nestling confidingly in its mother's bosom, be made to rise, by the blessing of the Holy Spirit, to a sublime height of love to God and man, and at last repose with perfect, unclouded affection upon the bosom of the heavenly Parent. "And," remarks Dr. Harris, "let the parents remember that from the moment they begin to point their child to God as an object of reverence and love, they are pursuing the certain course for augmenting its moral affection for themselves; while its intelligent love for them is a valuable means and pledge for its ascending to the love of God."

This affection, when rightly exercised, will display itself in expressions of gratitude for parental care and faithfulness, and in those numberless acts of kindness which the loving child will ever delight to render. It will prompt to a strict obedience, for the sake of affording pleasure to its objects, and sometimes will even incite to piety, rather than cause grief. This motive appears to have weighed powerfully upon the mind of "the judicious Hooker," who was accustomed to say, "If I had no other reason and motive for being religious, I would earnestly strive to be so *for the sake of my aged mother*, that I might requite her care of me, and cause the widow's heart to sing for joy."

Especially will it display itself in those kind attentions for which the age or infirmities of the parents often afford such opportunities. When the eyes that so lovingly watched over our early years become dim, and the hands that so tenderly nurtured us grow weak and trembling, when "the almond tree shall flourish, and the grasshopper shall be a burden," then the power of filial love will shine most brightly, and will eagerly render back something of that care to which it is so greatly indebted, yet which it can never wholly repay. That is a beautiful providence which so governs the family as thus to reverse its relative duties and dependencies, providing in the love of the child for the welfare of the aged and enfeebled parent, and rewarding his former faithfulness in duty by the corresponding fidelity of his offspring.

Not always, however, does the parent reap this delightful "fruit in old age." The selfishness of the human heart sometimes invades and mars even this sacred relation, and there are those—(may heaven pity them!)—who know

> "How sharper than a serpent's tooth it is
> To have a thankless child."

No form of ingratitude, save that of which God is the object, is so hateful and criminal as this. It betokens a hardness of heart, a deadness to all sense of duty and affection, which deserves, as it has received, the reprobation of mankind in all ages. It is a sin which seldom goes unpunished, even in this life. A wealthy man who for many years had allowed his widowed mother to depend upon the parish for support, and who at length consented to give her from his own purse the slight weekly pittance to which she had been accustomed, was made the subject of conversation in a circle of her friends, who proposed once more to remonstrate with him. "No," said an aged minister, "let him alone; if he dies possessed of the property he is now worth, I shall be deceived. God will never suffer such base ingratitude to prosper." In a short time afterwards, the mother was removed to another world. The circumstances of the son began to change, and though he had amassed his thousands, he was soon reduced to abject poverty.

Sometimes the sin of the ungrateful child recoils fearfully upon himself when he becomes a parent. A father was once emphatically reminded of this by his son. He had refused to support the grandfather of the child, and turned him out of the house. The old man said to his grandson, "Go and fetch the covering from my bed, that I may go and sit by the wayside and beg." The child burst into tears, and ran for the covering, having procured which, he said to his father, "Pray, father, cut it in two; the half of it will be large enough for grandfather, and perhaps you may want the other half when I grow to be a man, and turn you out of doors." The unnatural son was so affected by these words that he implored the forgiveness of his father, and was very kind to him till he died.

In happy contrast with these unlovely traits of character are those that often mark the Christian family, where the aged grand-parent goes gently down the decline of life, blessed by the tender sympathy and consideration of both old and young, being regarded by none as a burden, but fondly cherished and reverenced by all. The trials that are incident to old age are deprived of half their sting by the respect and forbearance of those around, and the absence of many other sources of joy is more than compensated by the delights of a happy fireside. Upon the other hand a golden return for this filial affection is poured into the bosoms of those who cherish it, in the lessons of practical wisdom and ripe experience that drop from the lips of age, as well as in the example furnished to the younger members of the family, by which they are likely to profit in after years. It cannot be doubted that children nurtured amid such influences are, of all others, the least likely to bring down the "gray hairs" of their own parents "in sorrow to the grave." Thus is filial piety ever its own abundant reward.

It may be added that the same spirit of love should characterize *the intercourse of children with each other.* Without it, the home can never be the happy spot that it is designed to be. That very closeness of relationship which adds a zest to the joys of affection, also greatly embitters the evils of hatred and discord. As a means of happiness, therefore, no less than as a dictate of duty, the most confiding sympathy should be cultivated by brothers and sisters. In every family there is much to be borne with upon all sides, and occasions frequently occur for the exercise of patience and forgiveness. When rightly improved, they become a healthful discipline, and tend to exercise and develop the kindlier dispositions of our nature. When met with an improper, unchristian spirit, they mar the peace of the household, and strengthen evil passions. It is therefore an important question with the young, who are just forming their habits for life, and taking the impress that shall perhaps mark them for eternity, whether, in the daily round of home intercourse, love or hatred, forbearance or anger, shall obtain the victory. Let none, however, rely upon any native amiability of disposition, as of itself sufficient to fulfil this obligation; but rather let all seek the animating influences of that religion, whose essence and whose fruit is love to God and our fellow-creatures. The home that is pervaded by the spirit of true piety will necessarily be marked by a holy affection, that is as delightful and profitable to ourselves as it is pleasing to God.

2. Another important filial duty is *respect for parents.* "Honour thy father and thy mother," is "the first commandment with promise;" Ex. xx. 12; Eph. vi. 2; and fearful are the curses denounced against him who disobeys it: "The eye that mocketh at his father, and despiseth to obey his mother, the ravens of the valley shall pick it out, and the young eagles shall eat it." Prov. xxx. 17.

But why is this duty so solemnly enjoined? Certainly it must be of the first importance, in order to be worthy of a place in the moral law. A little reflection will show that such is indeed the case. The family is the foundation of both the State and the Church; and whatever be the duties devolving upon us, either as citizens or Christians, the home is the school where we are to be trained for their discharge. For what is the State without a general respect for, and obedience to, its constituted authorities? Divested of this, the best form of government would degenerate into anarchy, and society would present a frightful spectacle of insubordination. Yet how can he who is accustomed to withhold the reverence due to his parents, be expected afterwards to honour the voice of civil law? The testimony of many a criminal, who has publicly referred his whole career of iniquity to his early failures in this particular, indicates what the entire social fabric would become, were the sentiment of filial reverence to be banished from the world.

Of still greater importance is this duty when viewed in its relation to the principles of true religion. God justly requires the adoring homage of his creatures, not only in his character of a King, but also in that of a *Father*, saying, "If I be a Father, *where is my honour?*" In the wise adaptations of the family constitution, he provides that this sentiment shall not be an unaccustomed one, even to the tenderest mind; and that thus, as soon as we are capable of understanding his claims, we shall, by the very force of previous habit, be the better prepared to obey them. The child who disregards the high and dignified position of his parents (whose voice is to him in infancy as the voice of God)—will have to pass through a severe ordeal, ere he can be brought to humble himself in the dust before his Maker. Upon the other hand, he who is accustomed to revere parental authority, when led by the Spirit to recognize that of his Creator, will be the better prepared to bow with holy awe before it, and to render that glory to the Divine name which is the proper object of his existence. We might pursue the thought farther, but enough has perhaps been said to show how wonderful are the bearings of the fifth commandment upon our social and religious well-being, and that it appropriately occupies the first place in the second table of the law.

The duty under consideration relates as well to thought and feeling as to conduct. It requires a deep, habitual esteem for one's parents, such as will not permit the child even to think lightly of them, much less in word or demeanour to show them disrespect. It likewise extends to *both* parents, the father and mother being distinctly specified in the Divine command. It is a remarkable circumstance that while the morality of the most cultivated ancient heathen nations has only required that children honour their father, the Divine law demands the honour of the *mother* also.

This feeling will find a thousand appropriate channels of expression; exhibiting itself in the daily conduct, in a ready obedience to the parental will, and a cheerful deference to its authority. Its influence will not be confined to the circle of the family, but it will become a powerful motive to right conduct in one's intercourse with the world. That is the best tribute of filial respect, which is rendered by the obedient life; and in no way can the child so honour a wise and faithful parent, as by illustrating in his own career the power of his instructions and example. It is mentioned by Miss Pardoe that a beautiful feature in the character of the Turks is reverence for their mother. "Their wives may reprimand unheeded, but their mother is an oracle, consulted, confided in, listened to with respect and deference, honoured to the latest hour, and remembered with affection and regret beyond the grave. 'Wives may die,' say they, 'and we can replace them; children perish, and others may be born to us; but who shall restore the mother, when she passes away and is seen no more?'"

There are many, and powerful *motives* to this duty, such as the acknowledged deference that is due from inferiors to superiors, the honourable position of the parents as the natural head of the family, and the claim that they have upon the respect of those for whom they have done so much; but we shall now confine ourselves to the motive employed by God himself, namely *the reward* of those who honour their parents. As expressed in the fifth commandment, it is in these words, "*that thy days may be long upon the land which the Lord thy God giveth thee.*"

This promise, no doubt, referred primarily, to God's chosen people, who were about to enter the land of Canaan. So literal, indeed, was its application to them, that when God threatened the nation with captivity in another land, the sin of dishonouring their parents was expressly mentioned as one cause of their calamity. "In thee have they set light by father and mother, * * * and I will scatter thee among the heathen, and disperse thee in the countries." Ezek. xxii. 7, 15. That neither the promise, however, nor its implied threatening, was confined to the Jewish people, is evident from its citation by the Apostle Paul: "Honour thy father and thy mother, (which is the first commandment with promise,) that it may be well with thee, and that thou mayest live long upon the earth." Eph. vi. 2, 3. Experience also proves that there is a special providence connected with the faithful discharge of filial duty, generally rewarding it with long life and temporal prosperity; and also that those who fail in this respect, do often come to an untimely end. As Philip Henry was once speaking of a wicked son in the neighbourhood, who was very undutiful to his mother, he charged some of his children to observe the providence of God concerning him. "Perhaps," said he, "I may not live to see it, but do you take notice whether God do not come upon him with some remarkable judgment in this life, according to the threatening implied in the reason annexed to the fifth commandment." He himself lived to see his words fulfilled, not long after, in a very signal providence. It seems only reasonable and natural that the transgressor of this command should thus reap the fruits of his impiety. For "the child is father to the man," and he who despises authority in the lesser sphere of the family, is not unlikely to do so in the broader one of society, and thus to be betrayed into crime and ignominy; while he who has early learned to defer to superior wisdom, and to control those passions which are the moving cause of filial irreverence, is likely to become a useful member of society, and to possess that virtue which tends to the prolongation of life, and the advancement of his temporal interest.

All are perhaps familiar with the conduct of Washington in this particular; yet as it so beautifully illustrates the nature and reward of filial respect, we cannot forbear quoting it. When quite young, he was about to go to sea as a midshipman. Everything was arranged; the vessel lay opposite his father's house, the little boat had come on shore to take him off, and his whole heart was bent on going. After his trunk had been carried down to the boat, he went to bid his mother farewell, and saw the tears bursting from her eyes. In an instant abandoning his cherished plans, he said to his servant, "Go and fetch my trunk back, *I will not go away to break my mother's heart.*" His mother, struck with his decision, exclaimed, "George, God has promised to bless the children that honour their parents, and I believe that he will bless you." And blessed he was by the grateful, affectionate, *filial* reverence of the multitudes who afterwards hailed him as "the father of his country." He who, despising that mother's tears, might afterwards have fought against his country's liberties, by yielding to their appeal, became its deliverer from bondage. We may not speak too decisively as to what God might or might not have done in his wonder-working providence, had Washington resolved differently upon that occasion; but in view of this remarkable circumstance, who shall say that the freedom achieved in the revolutionary war, and perpetuated to the millions who now enjoy it, is not, under God, a monument to the *filial piety* as well as the wise statesmanship of George Washington?

We need not multiply instances in support of a truth which is so uniformly illustrated in the experience of mankind. An intelligent observation of facts that daily transpire will convince the most sceptical upon this subject, that the Author of the command and promise which we have noticed is *the God of providence.* Let this motive, then, have its intended effect, and add its weight to the promptings of affection and of conscience, in inciting the young to honour their parents.

The promise of temporal reward, however, is not the only incentive to this duty. It is one that is intimately connected with the higher blessings of religion, and that is *essential to true piety.* This fact is recognized by the common sentiment of mankind. "It is remarkable," says a learned writer, "that while the duties owed to other men are termed justice, or charity, or courtesy, or liberality, or gratitude, those due to parents are, in most languages, comprised under the title of *piety.* Who, indeed, does not feel that it is something *more* than injustice to wrong a parent; that it is *more* than uncharitableness to refuse them succour or relief; that it is *more* than incivility to be unkind to them; that it is *more* than sordid avarice to withhold aid from their necessities? Who is not prompted at once to brand such conduct as *impiety?* Indeed the language of inspiration expressly confirms this view of the subject, "If any widow have children or nephews, (*i. e.* grand children,) let them first learn *to show piety at home*, and to requite their parents, for that is good and acceptable before God;" 1 Tim. v. 4; where the term employed is the proper one for expressing *piety* "towards God." * It is not, of course,

* Prof. Bush, on Ex. xx. 12.

meant by this that the honouring of one's parents is the whole of piety, but that it is one of its most pleasing and delightful as well as necessary fruits.

3. The duty of *obedience to parents* is so clearly implied in those that we have already considered, as to require no lengthened discussion. It is included in the meaning of the fifth commandment, and is enjoined with frequency and earnestness throughout the Scriptures. "Children, obey your parents in the Lord, for this is right." Eph. vi. 1. "Children, obey your parents in all things, for this is well pleasing unto the Lord." Col. iii. 20.

This obligation is founded in the relation of parents and children, and is universally recognized as a perfectly reasonable one. If it is the duty of parents to govern, the corresponding duty of children to obey follows as a matter of course. It is also implied in the position of the parents as the heaven-appointed guardians and educators of their offspring; it being very evident that the child who habitually disobeys them, is thereby defeating their kind efforts in his behalf, and thus depriving himself of the great blessings which it is their duty and desire to confer.

This obedience, to be acceptably rendered, should be *affectionate*, the dictate of love rather than of fear; should be *prompt*, not waiting for the second command, but yielded with cheerful alacrity—for "He twice obeys who obeys quickly;" should be *confiding*, even when the reason of the command is not fully understood, yet trusting in the superior wisdom of the parent; should be *uniform*, or rendered at all times, and extending to all duties, whether pleasurable or otherwise; and should be performed from a sense of *duty to God*, who so earnestly enjoins it, and in whose sight it is so "well pleasing." In those instances that sometimes occur, where the parental command is opposed to the word of God, the child ought clearly "to obey God rather than man;" yet in all such cases there is need of great caution, and we should be well satisfied that the thing required is as plainly forbidden by God, as filial obedience is commanded by him. When these two kinds of obligation do thus come into conflict, we are not warranted in withholding the respect due to the parent; but must treat him with kind regard, even when we cannot conscientiously obey.

A beautiful exhibition of this trait was once afforded by the Rev. Richard Cecil. When quite a little boy his father had occasion to go to a certain place, and took his son with him. While transacting business, he told his son to wait for him at the door; but forgetting him, he went out by another door, and returned home. In the evening the mother, missing her child, inquired where he was, when his father, suddenly recollecting his own directions to him, said, "You may depend upon it, he is still waiting where I appointed him." He immediately returned, and found his dear boy on the very spot where he had ordered him to remain. "He knew that his father expected him to wait, and therefore would not disappoint him."

Perhaps the sublimest display of filial obedience that the world has ever witnessed, (with the one exception of Him who, "though he were a son, yet learned obedience by the things which he suffered",) was that rendered by the youthful Isaac. We have no record of his submissive words when bound by his father's hands "on the altar upon the wood," for a burnt offering, nor when "Abraham stretched forth his hand and took the knife to slay his son;" yet the recorded fact that he was thus bound, and, to all human appearance, was about to be sacrificed, shows an obedience to parental authority which may well command our highest admiration. For he was not, as is so frequently represented, a mere child, but was probably at least twenty years of age, and no doubt strong and vigorous. He therefore could not have been bound against his will by Abraham, who was now an hundred and twenty-five years old; but must have yielded without resistance to the command of his father, and resigned himself submissively to the Divine will concerning him. As Dr. Kitto justly observes, "he was grown to strength and manhood, and if he had thought fit to struggle for his life, we cannot doubt that he might easily, without violence, have escaped from his father's hands, and fled away." The fact of there being no recorded conversation between them at this juncture enhances the lustre of his obedience; for perhaps he would spare his afflicted father the pain of a single reproach, and forbear inflicting another pang upon his already breaking heart, by those appeals which he might naturally have made. Be this as it may, he must have "*offered* his hands and feet to the cords, his bosom to the knife, his body to the altar" in obedience to the paternal will. If the part of Abraham in this transaction was a victory of faith, so was that of Isaac a victory of filial piety, and the strength of the one scarcely surpassed that of the other.

As this duty is implied in the requirement of the fifth commandment, so the blessing there set forth must be regarded as attending its faithful discharge. Many an one can distinctly trace his prosperity in life, both temporal and spiritual, to his early habits of filial obedience. The excellent mother of Dr. Timothy Dwight declared a short time before her death, that she did not know the instance in which her son had ever disobeyed a parental command, or failed in the performance of a filial duty! That son, as is well known, rose to a position of great honour and influence, and was made a rich blessing to the church and the world. Upon the other hand, many a ruined wretch can discern the first steps of his downward career in the disobedient acts of his childhood. It was once stated at a meeting of the American Prison Discipline Society, as the result of the examinations made by that institution, into the history and career of the various criminals confined in the prisons of the United States, that "*in almost all cases* their course of ruin began in *disobedience to parents*. This was followed by intemperance, and that made way for all other crimes."

The light in which *God* regards this sin is shown in his command to the Israelites, "If a man have a stubborn and rebellious son, which will not obey the voice of his father, or the voice of his mother, and that, when they have chastened him, will not hearken unto them; then shall his father and his mother lay hold on him, * * * and they shall say to the elders of the city, 'This our son is stubborn and rebellious, he will not obey our voice; he is a glutton and a drunkard;' and all the men of Israel shall stone him with stones, that he die." Deut. xxi. 18—21. Under the milder laws of the Christian dispensation, we are indeed spared the necessity of such extreme punishment; yet this ancient law evinces the Divine horror of filial rebellion, and shows that however the child may be disposed to regard it, it is, in the eye of God, a *crime* of no ordinary magnitude.

Like every other form of sin, this one has its *first steps*, against which both parents and children ought sedulously to guard. It may appear a slight thing to the wayward youth to resist, for once, the voice of parental authority, but let him reflect that, like the first glass of the drunkard, or the first oath of the blasphemer, it is likely to be the beginning of a downward course which will ruin his character and destroy his happiness; and which, besides causing grief to the hearts that love him, may turn the scale of his eternal destiny. So, also, it may seem but a slight thing to obey "in all things;" but every act of true obedience strengthens and confirms the habit, and throws around the heart the safeguards of virtue, and forms one of the best preparations for, as it is one of the most delightful fruits of piety.

There is implied in this duty a disposition to yield to the *instructions*, no less than the commands, of parents. Says the wise man, "My son, hear the instruction of thy father, and forsake not the law of thy mother; for they shall be an ornament of grace unto thy head, and chains about thy neck." Prov. i. 8, 9. And this kind of obedience is not only graceful, but also highly profitable, tending as well to our greater security as to our guidance in right and pleasant paths; "When thou goest, it shall lead thee; when thou sleepest, it shall keep thee; and when thou wakest, it shall talk with thee." Prov. vi. 22. The teachings of the faithful parent are intended to promote the best welfare of the child for time and eternity. He who listens to them may not at the time comprehend all their bearings upon his happiness, and they may appear irksome to the unrenewed heart; yet, if not heeded, the time will come when they will be seen in their true character, though it may be too late, alas! to profit by them. The slighting of parental counsels is not only sin, but—as is indeed the case with all sin—is absolute folly. Such is the declaration of God's word, "*A fool* despiseth his father's instruction." Happy are they who have attained in early life to the wisdom of a docile spirit, and who are led by the simple lessons of childhood to sit at the feet of Jesus and hear his words. In them are fulfilled the assurances of Divine Wisdom, "I love them that love me, and they that seek me early shall find me." "For whoso findeth me findeth life, and shall obtain favour of the Lord. But," it is added, "he that sinneth against me wrongeth his own soul: all they that hate me love death." Prov. viii. 17, 35, 36.

It is, however, not enough simply to give the attention of the mind to parental teachings. They fail of their true effect, unless they also move the heart, and control the life. The obedience required by God is not alone that of hearing or reciting lessons of heavenly truth, nor the mere storing of the memory with words of wisdom, but the securing of that great end for which the family is ordained, and which both parents and children should alike have in view, *the conversion of the young to God.* As no instruction is thorough which has not this for its object, so no obedience is complete that is satisfied with anything less than this. The child or youth who enjoys the prayers and counsels of pious parents is, by that very circumstance, laid under an added obligation to give his heart to God, and seek his personal salvation; and fearful are his responsibilities if he neglects this sacred duty. For, awful as will be the situation of every impenitent sinner at the last day, surely his guilt will be the deepest, who has thus sinned against the most light, and neglected the best opportunities. And we may well believe that his misery will be proportionably aggravated. For, next to the thought of having despised the love of God in Christ, there can be no reflections more harrowing to the lost soul than those that are associated with its early, yet unheeded instructions in piety, with the despised counsels of a father, or the prayers and tears of a fond mother, and all the hallowed, yet, alas! unregarded influences of a Christian home.

The motives to early piety are many: such as its being commanded by God, and its being more easily attained, more pleasing to our Maker, more delightful to ourselves, and more useful to the church and the world than any other; but we may urge as a consideration that ought not to be overlooked, that it is a duty owed to those parents, who have consecrated their offspring to God in infancy, and who labour and pray for their conversion. The claims of our Creator do, indeed, transcend those of any creature in importance; but he is pleased to link them in with those of parental affection, thus strengthen-

8

ing the cords by which he would draw us to himself. We therefore appeal to the youthful reader, who has been nurtured amid such sacred influences, to heed the voice which not only addresses him from the throne and the heart of God, but from the lips of beloved parents who are drawing near the grave, or who, perhaps, are already sainted: "*Remember now thy Creator in the days of thy youth!*"

CHAPTER V.

DUTIES AND RESPONSIBILITIES OF MASTERS AND SERVANTS.

IV. A FOURTH class of duties belonging to the family relation are those of *masters and servants.*

The gospel, while recognizing the essential equality of the brotherhood of man, does not ignore the inequality of condition and circumstances that so widely exists. While regarding all classes of men as upon a level in respect to their spiritual interests, being involved in the same guilt, and included in the same offers of mercy, whether "Jews or Gentiles, bond or free," it at the same time furnishes rules of duty for the king and the subject, the rich and the poor, the master and the servant. And it cannot be doubted that religion, in aiming to sanctify and govern the relations *that naturally exist* among men, accomplishes a far nobler work, than if its endeavours were directed to the equalizing, upon an unnatural basis, of the whole human family. It does not indulge in impracticable theories of a perfect social state, while men are imperfect, and, in general, unregenerate; but rather assigns those duties that shall evolve out of every sphere of life the highest good of those connected with it, wisely directing and governing that which is imperfect, until "that which is perfect is come," and "that which is in part shall be done away."

The relation of master and servant has existed from the earliest antiquity, and must be regarded as an essential part of the family constitution. It is founded upon that wise provision of the Divine government, by which the labour of the poor receives its equivalent from the means of those more favoured in temporal things than themselves. Its principle is therefore the same with that of any other department of labour, such as manufacture, or barter, or the services of the professional man; with the exceptions that the toils of the servant are generally limited to the demands of one household, and that his station is, from the nature of the case, one of subjection and social inferiority. In these respects, however, the words and example of Jesus have ennobled the position of those who faithfully serve: "I am among you as he that serveth." "He made himself of no reputation, and took on him the form of a servant."

The duties and responsibilities of this relation are various and important, and are set forth in the Scriptures with a degree of clearness that can leave no doubt as to the light in which they are regarded by our Maker.

1. The first duty of THE MASTER, and one from which nothing can exonerate him, is *justice* to those who are engaged in his service. "Masters, give unto your servants that which is just and equal; knowing that ye also have a Master in heaven." Col. iv. 1. Among the requirements of the Mosaic law, we read, "Thou shalt not

oppress a hired servant that is poor and needy, whether he be of thy brethren, or of thy strangers that are in thy land within thy gates. At his day thou shalt give him his hire, neither shall the sun go down upon it; for he is poor and setteth his heart upon it; lest he cry against thee unto the Lord, and it be sin unto thee." Deut. xxiv. 14, 15.

Of all forms of injustice, scarcely any is more criminal in itself, or more disastrous in its consequences, than that of which the poor are the subjects. Dependent upon their hard earned wages for support, and often debarred by their scanty means, or ignorance, or fear, from obtaining legal redress, or protecting themselves against fraud, they may well lay claim to the sympathy, and much more to the honesty, of those with whom they have to deal. He who is just, will not only avoid defrauding them in a pecuniary point of view, but will also be careful to exact no more labour from them than they can reasonably be required to render. The obligation, "As ye would that others should do to you, do ye even so to them," is as applicable to this as to every other relation in life. The gospel makes no exception, and we can make none. God, who "judgeth the poor and the needy," has evinced his jealous care for them in terrible woes pronounced against oppressive masters: "I will come near to you to judgment, and I will be a swift witness against * * * those that oppress the hireling in his wages, the widow and the fatherless." Mal. iii. 5. Says an apostle, "Behold the hire of the labourers, who have reaped your fields, which is of you kept back by fraud, crieth: and the cries of them which have reaped are entered into the ears of the Lord of Sabaoth." James v. 4. But we need not dwell at length upon a duty that is so obviously demanded by the voice of conscience and morality, and the laws of God and man.

Mere justice, however, though it be rigidly practised, can never fulfil the whole of human obligation in regard to any of our fellow beings. Of equal importance with this is the duty of *love*, in its various forms of benevolence, compassion, kindness, and forbearance. This duty is indeed required by justice itself, for love is rather a debt that we owe, than a favour we may render, as is plain from the apostle's words, "*Owe* no man any thing, but *to love one another*."

The head of an earthly household, like the "Master in heaven," has to do with imperfect, sinful creatures, and therefore finds frequent occasion for the exercise of clemency. When we consider, moreover, that the earthly master, unlike the heavenly, is himself a frail, fallible being, and a servant of the most High, we have an added motive to an imitation of the Divine example. For how can he look with confidence for mercy from God, who withholds it from his fellow men? The apostle Paul employs this as a motive to kindness: "And ye masters, do the same thing unto them, forbearing threatening, knowing that *your Master also is in heaven*, neither is there respect of persons with him." Eph. vi. 9. The exercise of kindness and forbearance is so far from being inconsistent with a proper maintenance of authority, that it rather adds to its real weight, and secures a cheerful acquiescence in its claims. That servant is generally the most faithful who is the most attached to the master.

Thus interest unites with duty, in bidding us make the law of kindness the law of the household.

Instances are by no means rare in which this relationship is pervaded by a beautiful affection, the faithful servant having a place in the hearts of parents and children, and being, in turn, devotedly attached to them and all their interests. The trials incident to their lot are lightened by a mutual confidence and esteem; and as they grow old, they for whom their best days have been spent, delight in rendering them kind attentions, and when they die, they are mourned as beloved friends. A most touching instance of such affectionate fidelity upon the part of a servant, is related of a negro woman in Hayti. During the occurrence of a dreadful earthquake, the inmates had all fled from one of the falling houses, leaving this woman, who was the nurse, with her master's infant child. She would not desert her charge, though the walls were even then giving way; but with a noble heroism, extended her bended form across its body, where she was found crushed to death by the fallen roof, the child lying unharmed beneath her.

Especially let those of our dependents who are of "the household of faith," be regarded with tender consideration; as Paul bid Philemon receive the converted Onesimus, "not now as a servant, but above a servant, a brother beloved." Where the servant is not a disciple of Christ, the faithful master will labour and pray for his conversion. His obligation so to do flows naturally from his position of influence and authority. Indeed his responsibility in this respect is similar to that which he sustains towards his children. For although these relations differ widely, yet they are alike in this, that the servant as well as the child is providentially entrusted to his keeping, to be trained for the Divine glory. The purpose of the family constitution must be regarded as having reference to *every member of the household*, whether they be kindred, friends, or servants. It should be the case that for any person to reside temporarily within the influences of the Christian home, would be synonymous with breathing an atmosphere of piety, and engaging to some degree in the duties of religion.

Such was undoubtedly the case in patriarchal times. God said of Abraham, "I know that he will command his children *and his household* after him, and they shall keep the way of the Lord, to do justice and judgment." Gen. xviii. 19. Upon which Matthew Henry remarks: "Abraham not only took care of his children, but of his household; his servants were catechized servants. Masters of families should instruct and inspect the manners of all under their roof. The poorest servants have precious souls that must be looked after." When Jacob, at the command of God, was about to go to Beth-el for the purpose of building an altar to Jehovah, he "said unto *his household, and all that were with him*, Put away the strange gods that are among you, and be clean, and change your garments, and let us arise and go to Bethel, and I will make there an altar unto God." Gen. xxxv. 2, 3. This would seem to indicate that servants must be required to attend upon family worship, and, wherever practicable, follow the master to the house of God. That the strict observance of *the Sabbath* is to be enforced upon them, is plain from the terms of the fourth commandment: "In it thou shalt not do any work, thou, nor thy son, nor thy daughter, nor *thy man-servant, nor thy maid-servant.*" In the reiteration of the ten commandments in the book of Deuteronomy, we find this duty yet more strongly enjoined, it being added, "that thy man-servant and thy maid-servant may rest as well as thou; and remember that thou wast a servant in the land of Egypt." Deut. v. 14, 15. The affairs of the household should be arranged in reference to this requirement, that the duties of those who serve may be as light as is possible upon that sacred day. It is very evident that they who devote holy Sabbath hours to unnecessary feasting, or the entertainment of friends, violate the very letter of the law.

We are informed that Cornelius the Centurion "feared God with all his house, " a commendation that is full of significance; for, being an officer of high rank, he must have had many servants, all of whom, we may infer, were like "the devout soldier of them that waited on him continually," (Acts x. 47,) whom he sent to Joppa. That is a blessed household of which as much as this can be said, and all of whose members, from the highest to the lowest, are united in the fear and service of the Divine Master. Such no doubt, was the family of David, who said, "He that walketh in a perfect way, he shall serve me. He that worketh deceit shall not dwell within my house." Ps. ci. 6, 7. Such also was the family of Joshua, who declared, "As for me and my house, we will serve the Lord."

The proper means of promoting the spiritual welfare of those thus committed to his charge, will readily occur to the Christian master. Besides those efforts that are more direct, such as instruction and counsel, there is great power in a consistent, holy life, and an habitual recognition of God in the intercourse of the family. These, with the manifestation of a tender solicitude for their conversion, and the use of the proper instrumentalities, will seldom fail of impressing their minds, and may be blessed by the Holy Spirit to their salvation.

In addition to the fact of the master's responsibility, and the value of the souls whom we may thus be instrumental in converting, there is another motive to this duty which ought not to be overlooked: namely, *the influence of servants over other members of the family*, and especially over the minds of the young. While every mother should be careful that the early culture of her children be not left to a mere hireling, there yet will be frequent occasions when they are under the care of the servant, whose words and conduct they will insensibly imitate. So powerful is the influence thus exerted, that in some families the dispositions and habits of the young are moulded to a greater degree by the nurse than by the parent. Supposing, however, that parental duty is faithfully discharged, is it not an obligation owed to one's children, to secure, as far as is practicable, piety in those with whom they are thrown so much in contact? If the gardener will see to it that none shall tend his plants and trees, who are likely to bring hurtful influences to bear upon them, and impede their growth, how much more should the Christian parent study the piety of those who have so much to do in rearing his precious offspring! A celebrated preacher, being taunted with the remark that his large congregation was chiefly made up of servants and low people, replied, "I know it is; my church is made up of such converts as Jesus Christ and his apostles gained—and as for servants, I had rather be instrumental in converting them than their employers, *because they have the care of all the children.*"

2. The duties of the SERVANT correspond with those of the master. If the one must be just, the other is required to be *obedient and faithful.* "Servants, be obedient to them that are your masters according to the flesh, with fear and trembling, in singleness of your heart, as unto Christ; not with eye-service, as men-pleasers, but as the servants of Christ, doing the will of God from the heart." Eph. vi. 5, 6.

Neither the demands nor the promises of religion are confined to any particular sphere of life. The position of the king is not so high, nor that of the beggar so low, as to exclude them from its pale, or absolve them from its obligations. The possessor of one talent was held equally accountable in fact, though not in degree, with him who had five; and, be the circle of one's influence great or small, it must be filled to its outer boundary with the faithful performance of its appropriate duties. The fidelity of those in low stations to their appointed trusts is equally honourable to themselves, and acceptable to God, with the obedient service of others "to whom much is given," and of whom "much will be required." That this is the case, and that God looks rather at our fidelity in the sphere he has allotted us, than at what we might possibly have done in some other one from which in his providence we are debarred, is plain from the Master's commendation of the faithful servant: "Thou hast been faithful over a few things, I will make thee ruler over many things; enter thou into the joy of thy Lord." Matt. xxv. 21. The principle upon which this plaudit is founded is elsewhere set forth in the words: "He that is faithful in that which is least, is faithful also in much: and he that is unjust in the least, is unjust also in much." Luke xvi. 10. It follows from this, that the duties of the servant are by no means unimportant, and that his obligations are as binding, and his conscientious discharge of them as acceptable as those of any other person.

Unfortunate, then, as may seem the lot of those who, by reason of poverty, are reduced to a state of subjection to others, and to persons no better by nature than themselves, it yet becomes them to be thankful that their bodily wants are thus cared for, and obediently to serve those whom Providence has made their employers. It belongs to the very relation existing between them that the master command, and the servant obey, and the service thus rendered is ennobled by the gospel into a religious duty. Of course, when the thing commanded is unlawful, or contrary to the word of God, the servant, like the child, "ought to obey God rather than man." Instances have been known in which the conscientiousness of the servant in this particular has been overruled for the good of the master and his household. Thus Dr. Jay relates that a servant who had attended a Wesleyan chapel, greatly to the offence of her employers, was told that she must discontinue the practice, or leave their service. She received the information with modesty, and said she was sorry, but so it must be; she could not sacrifice the convictions of her conscience to keep her place. Having received warning to leave, she resolved to be more circumspect and exemplary than ever—being determined that if she suffered for her religion, her religion should not suffer for her. Upon reflection, she was permitted to remain, and such was her exhibition of the power of true godliness, that her mistress at length said to her husband, "I think that Mary's religion seems to do her a great deal more good than our religion seems to do us; I should like to hear her minister." They went together for that purpose, both were impressed, and became followers of God, and they set up the family altar in their house.

But supposing that the master is unreasonable and tyrannical in his demands—is it still duty to obey? Undoubtedly, if the way be not open for exchanging his service for that of one more kind, religion demands submission to his authority. Says the apostle Peter, "Servants, be subject to your masters with all fear; not only to the good and gentle, but also to the froward, for this is thankworthy, if a man for conscience towards God endure grief, suffering wrongfully. For what glory is it if, when ye be buffeted for your *faults*, ye take it patiently? But if, when ye *do well and suffer for it*, ye take it patiently, this is acceptable with God." 1 Pet. ii. 18–20.

It is indeed hard to submit in silence to the indignities that are sometimes heaped upon the head of the faithful servant, to "answer not again," and to yield an uncomplaining obedience to the caprices of a petty tyrant; yet rarely does religion shine so brightly as when it thus triumphs. Dr. Chalmers eloquently remarks, "The long-suffering of a Christian servant may in these circumstances look a tame and pusillanimous thing to those who look at it with this world's eyes, and pass their judgment on it upon the world's principles; but I am quite sure that in the high estimate of eternity, a servant never makes a greater exhibition of character, or reaches to a nearer resemblance of the Godhead himself, than when he comes off a conqueror from such a trial of the charity that 'endureth'—and when I put him by the side of the fretful oppressor, who is either so unprincipled as to defraud him, or so outrageous as to be ever and anon pursuing him with his restless and vindictive effusions, neither my reverence for his superior wealth, nor for the chair of little brief authority on which he sits, can restrain me from offering to the attendant who toils beside him, the tribute of a more honourable testimony, and the homage of a profounder reverence."

Perhaps the one duty of the servant that includes all others, the general rule that should regulate all his intercourse with his master, is contained in those precepts which enjoin serving "*in the fear of God,*" and discharging his obligations "as to the Lord, and not unto men," "as the servants of Christ, doing the will of God from the heart." Col. iii. 22, 23; Eph. vi. 6. In other words, he is not to forget that the eye of the Divine Master is upon him, and that a Divine authority obliges him to a conscientious obedience to that human authority to which he is, for the time, subjected. He should serve from higher motives than those of self-interest.

The claims of religion press equally upon him and his master, and it is as much the duty of the one to obey, as it is that of the other to command, "in the fear of God." He who is thus actuated by religious principle will labour with cheerful fidelity. The consciousness of glorifying his Maker will add a zest to his most trivial duties, and the consolations of the gospel will sustain him under his sorest trials, as he rejoices in being a partaker of that grace, "where there is neither Greek nor Jew, circumcision nor uncircumcision, Barbarian, Scythian, *bond nor free*, but *Christ is all and in all.*"

CHAPTER VI.

THE BEST MEANS OF SECURING THE END DESIGNED.

In the government of God there is a necessary connection and proportion between the means and the end. So true is this, that it may safely be assumed of any required duty that the means are at hand for its fulfilment. Our heavenly Father is not like the Egyptian taskmaster, requiring "bricks without straw," or duty without opportunity. If he bids us work in his vineyard, he furnishes the moral implements for its culture; if he requires that we display beneficence, he provides both its means and its objects; if he commands us to preach the gospel, he gives the voice to speak, the ear to hear, and the mind and heart to be impressed. Having seen the duties involved in the family relation, and the end which it is intended to subserve, the training of immortal souls for the Divine service and glory, the question may well occur, how shall this high purpose be best accomplished? What are the means and adaptations lodged in the bosom of the family, which we may seize and apply to this holy end? It will be shown, as we proceed, that

God has furnished us with all that could be desired in this respect, and has endowed the parent with a wealth of influences and opportunities, that afford the greatest encouragement to faithfulness, and leave him without excuse who fails to improve them.

1. As a necessary preparative to the diligent and successful use of these means, it is of the first importance that the parent *endeavour fully to realize his responsibility.* This cannot easily be over estimated. No human mind can grasp it in all its length and breadth; for we are finite creatures, and the issues of our conduct may be infinite and eternal. Yet who can contemplate, without a shudder, the thought of standing at the great tribunal, amid the family group that now surrounds him, and there answering to the Judge of quick and dead for the manner in which he has discharged his trust as their teacher and guide in Divine things? More than all, who can endure the thought of there witnessing the dreadful doom of even one of those who now gladden his home and enliven his heart, with the consciousness that it is the bitter fruit of his unfaithfulness, and that their blood shall be required at his hands?

Awful as is this responsibility, it rests upon every parent. It is implied in his very position and office, as well as in the whole tenor of the Divine requirements in regard to him. It may be treated with indifference, or lost sight of in the giddy round of business or pleasure, or the attempt may be made to transfer it to others; but it can no more be thrown off, than one can cease to be a parent, or can annul the whole course of God's moral government. Despite all efforts at evasion, it must ever rest where God has placed it—a fixed, inviolable ordination of Jehovah, a basis of duty here, and of judgment hereafter.

Solemn thought! that besides those invisible cords that bind parent and child in a common love and joy, they are also mysteriously united, while yet distinct and separate, in their accountability to their Maker! that the precious gift of God which the fond mother clasps lovingly to her bosom, not only brings with it a new world of delights, but a tremendous burden of responsibilities! What reflections may well crowd upon the mind that is conscious of such a trust as a young immortal, looking up to him as its law and example, and taking from him its lasting habits of thought, feeling, and action, while he stands between it and God, the representative of the Creator, the dispenser towards it of a moral government resembling the Divine! Well may the parent tremble as he contemplates all this, and cry from the depths of an anxious heart: "Who is sufficient for these things?" Well may such a view inspire his noblest endeavours, and impel him to a reliance upon that grace which alone can sustain him under it.

Yet how often is this aspect of the parental relation almost or quite overlooked! It seems strange indeed that so many of those who practically recognize their duty to feed and clothe and educate their families, can forget their higher obligations to afford them spiritual culture, and to clothe their souls with the robe of the Saviour's righteousness. They involuntarily obey that human law which devolves upon them the temporal support of their offspring; but are the claims of the Divine law of less importance than the human? What a pitiable folly do they exhibit, who lavish their attentions upon the dying bodies of their children, at the expense of their souls, and degrade the high and holy office of the parent into that of a minister to youthful vanity, or a weak ambition! How sublime, upon the other hand, the position of him who devotes his best energies to the task of moulding a young heart into a temple of the living God, and giving a right direction to those powers which shall survive the body's dissolution, and be drawn out to all eternity in the love and praise of God! The one is building his house upon the sand, the other upon a rock. The course of the one is inglorious and criminal, that of the other is godlike.

And let it be borne in mind, that if the responsibilities of the parent are vast, so too, if he be faithful, are *his joys.* No words can paint the rapture of him who welcomes to the "Father's house" one and another of the offspring whom God has given him, and finds in their endless happiness the reward of grace that has crowned his feeble endeavours. He who would realize such a blessedness hereafter, must now realize his responsibilities. Oh that they might so weigh upon every parent's mind and heart as to impel them to an earnest, conscientious discharge of their sacred trust! We are indeed inadequate to its perfect fulfilment, and he is sure to fail who undertakes it in his own strength; but the voice of Him who has imposed it addresses us in words of delightful encouragement, "*My grace is sufficient for thee.*"

2. Having allowed to this and kindred considerations their due weight, and with the whole heart wrought up

to a holy resolution, the parent should diligently employ those *means* that seem best adapted to promote religion in the family; of these, one of the most important is to *begin early.*

The susceptibility of early childhood to instruction and example renders it the period most favourable to implanting seeds of Divine truth, and forming character for eternity. Indeed, as a moral being, the child cannot but be influenced for good or evil by surrounding circumstances, nor can the parent help impressing him. So that the real question is, not whether he shall begin early to educate him—that is already decided by the Divine appointment—but whether that early training which he must, unavoidably, carry on, shall have a right or wrong direction; whether it shall be marked by the presence or the absence of religion. Says a writer, "Some parents talk of *beginning* the education of their children: the moment they were capable of forming an idea, their education was already begun—the education of circumstances—insensible education, which, like insensible perspiration, is of more constant and powerful effect, and of far greater consequence to the habit than that which is direct and apparent. This education goes on at every instant of time—you can neither stop it nor turn its course. * * * Here, then, is one school from which there are no truants, and in which there are no holidays."

A mental philosopher has said that character is formed before the expiration of the sixth year of our existence. It cannot be doubted that such is generally the case. Instances, indeed, there are in which Divine grace triumphs over defects of education as well as those of nature, and imparts in after years a character the opposite of that which is possessed in childhood; but these are exceptional cases. It is the testimony of experience that the child, like the young plant, takes on the form and direction of its whole life, from which it will be difficult to turn when it has reached maturity. Most parents readily acknowledge this fact; but perhaps many cherish erroneous views as to the *proper period* of beginning to inculcate the truths and duties of religion, and thus allow the season of greatest opportunity to go by unimproved. We therefore urge the importance of impressing even the *infant* mind in Divine things. As soon as the child is capable of receiving or comprehending an idea, let that idea be of God, of Christ, of heaven. Let religion be taught as the first and most important lesson of life, and it will be likely to cling to the heart with a power that we can hardly realize. If, as Richter says, "every first thing continues for ever with the child; the first colour, the first music, the first flower, paint the foreground of life," how necessary it is that that which is of the greatest moment to a human being should occupy the most prominent place among his early impressions!

It is the opinion of some, although it is not, we believe, as widely cherished as formerly, that *very young children* are not to be expected to manifest real piety; that they cannot comprehend the truths and doctrines of the Bible, or realize their individual accountability. Perhaps the perceptions of the infant mind may be clearer than is generally imagined; but be this as it may, the affections of the young heart are certainly *no less* adapted than those of the older and more hardened, to the reception and practice of the religion of *love*. And what if the child be not versed in all the mysteries of theological lore? He can *exercise* saving faith, even when he cannot define it, and can confide in his heavenly Father's word, without the medium of human argument as to its genuineness and authenticity. He can obey the Saviour's invitation, and come to him, and be pressed to his kind bosom, while the man of learning waits to ponder some abstruse point of doctrine, or to reconcile some difficulty of revelation.

That there is something in the little child that is in harmony with the spirit of piety, something that renders him the more hopeful a subject of renewing grace, is evident from our Saviour's words, "Except ye be converted, and become *as little children*, ye shall not enter into the kingdom of heaven." Matt. xviii. 3. Is it probable that our Lord would select, as a type of some of the essential features of his religion, those who were at the same time incapable of embracing it? But his own authority, upon another occasion, sets this question at rest. In rebuking the officiousness of his disciples, who would have kept young children from him, he seems to have particularly guarded against the error we are noticing. Instead of saying that *the young*, or *children* could come to him, terms which might have been regarded as indefinite, he takes them up in his arms — (a circumstance which shows that they were quite small)—and says, "Suffer *little children* to come unto me, and forbid them not, for of such is the kingdom of heaven." Mark

x. 4. Then hesitate not, O Christian parent, to bring your "little children" to Jesus, nor, by cherishing false views of their fitness, "forbid" them the joys and blessings of early piety. If the Saviour bids them come, it is not for the parent, by his neglect or procrastination, to keep them back.

Perhaps we might learn a lesson upon this subject from the idolaters of India. It is said that the first effort of the Hindoo mother, as soon as her child can speak, is to teach it to lisp the name of its god. A missionary, who was once describing a religious procession in Madras, stated that as it passes slowly through the streets, with the idol borne in front, and elevated above the heads of the people, mothers may be seen rushing from the surrounding houses, with their babes in their arms, and then holding them up and directing their eyes to the image, with expressions of the profoundest reverence. And will any say that the pure, simple truths of Christianity are less adapted to the mind of infancy, or less capable of impressing it, than the doctrines of Hindooism?

Modern biography has confirmed the teaching of the Scriptures in regard to the possibility and appropriateness of very early piety, and some of its most delightful pages are adorned with exemplifications of this truth. Instances are by no means unfrequent, in which children of but three or four years old have given good evidence of conversion, and afterwards confirmed it by the testimony of consistent Christian lives. Not to quote from the many narratives with which the Christian public are already familiar, we give the following touching extract from a recently published letter upon the subject, by the Rev. Dr. Plumer. "'What do you do without a mother to tell all your troubles to?' asked a child who had a mother, of one who had not; her mother was dead. 'Mother told me whom to go to before she died,' answered the little orphan. 'I go to the Lord Jesus; he was mother's friend and he is mine.' 'Jesus Christ is up in the sky,' said the other; 'he is away off, and has a great many things to attend to in heaven. It is not likely he can stop to mind you.' 'I do not know any thing about that,' said the orphan; 'all I know is, *he says he will, and that's enough for me.*' The little child was right. Jesus Christ was once a little child. He remembers, and knows how to minister to the sorrows of childhood as well as those of riper years. It is not six months since a little child, not three years old, when dying, said to its parents; 'Papa, Mamma, don't cry; I am going *home.*' Who can doubt that Christ is with such little sufferers! Why should it be thought a thing incredible that the great Shepherd should be very tender, and peculiarly near to his dear little lambs?"

Were this truth more generally believed and recognized, it cannot be questioned that one important barrier to parental fidelity and success would be removed. We need more *faith* in the word and promise of the Saviour; a faith such as will not dare assign limits to the operations of his grace, nor say of any whom he has invited to himself, that they are too young, or too weak to serve him. Might not the sentence be appropriately inscribed over many a Christian home, "He did not many mighty works there, because of their unbelief?" We commend these thoughts to the prayerful attention of every parent.

3. As a further means of promoting family religion, *the home should be made pleasant and happy.*

If the Christian home is a type of heaven, and a school where souls are to be trained for its enjoyment, it is but reasonable to conclude that it should be pervaded by a semblance of heaven's delights. True religion, while sober, is at the same time cheerful; and *family* religion, if it be genuine and scriptural, will possess the same characteristics. In urging, therefore, that the home be rendered attractive to those who dwell in it, we simply recommend that the claims of piety be cultivated, and religion allowed to exercise its genial sway, and diffuse its gladdening influences. A happy childhood, passed in a Christian home, is an inestimable blessing; for the memories of our early years are the last to leave us; and when thus associated with the delights of piety, they form through life a winning and powerful plea for the blessedness of serving God. The wanderer from virtue's paths, who has become hardened against every other influence, cannot forget his peaceful childhood's hours, and their crowding memories are sometimes blessed as the means of impelling him to that religion which constituted one of their principal charms. Upon the other hand, he has much to contend with, whose early recollections of religion are associated with a gloomy, repulsive home, and the forbidding aspect of stern authority. For the honour of Christianity, then, no spot where it is claimed to have rule should be cheerless and joyless. The heart is naturally arrayed in sufficient opposition to it, without being thus prejudiced against its claims.

Especially ought we to guard against surrounding *the young* with such influences as will lead them to think that piety and happiness are necessarily opposed to each other. Children are endowed with a strong appetite for enjoyment, and God intended that it should be gratified to a reasonable degree, and with legitimate delights; and while encouraged in their innocent pastimes, they should early be taught the "pleasantness" of wisdom's ways. Upon this subject, mere lip instruction will not suffice. It should be confirmed by the example of all around; should beam in the parent's eye, and glow in his smile, and be daily, hourly breathed in the atmosphere of home, until it is seen to be an all-pervading principle, that extends to every duty and trial, and is illustrated in every incident. Such an influence as this is hard to resist, and he who is favoured with it in early life, is the more likely to become, by the Divine blessing, a happy Christian.

It is also an important fact, which many a parent has learned to his sorrow, when too late to remedy it, that *if happiness be not found at home, it is sure to be sought elsewhere.* Our streets are filled with those who seek in the company of the vicious and profligate the enjoyment from which they are debarred in the more safe, but sometimes uncongenial, society of the family. Said a prisoner to a missionary who visited him in his cell, "It was my *street-education* that ruined me. I used to slip out of the house, and go off with the boys in the street. In the street I learned to lounge; in the street I learned to swear, to smoke, to gamble, to pilfer. Oh, sir! it is in the street the devil lurks to work the ruin of the young."

Let, then, the home be made the most attractive spot in the world to its occupants—the magnet, towards which their desires and affections shall ever tend. Let its pure pleasures sweeten the hours of childhood, and even become a safeguard against temptation, when they are exchanged for the excitements of more active life. There need be no sacrifice of principle, no conflicting with duty, in order to attain this end; nor are we warranted in resorting to sinful sources of amusement as a means of securing it. Let affection become the law of the household, and each one aim at contributing his share to the common fund of happiness; let the parents interest themselves in the little joys of their children; and while firm in duty, be kind and gentle in demeanour; and more than all, let the sacred delights of piety be assiduously cherished—and a spell is woven around the young heart which cannot easily be broken. Not only is the child thus held, as with cords of love, within the sphere of parental influence, until his habits are correctly formed; but he grows up with juster views of the blessedness of piety, and is the better prepared to embrace that religion which is not only instilled into his mind, but so beautifully illustrated before his eyes.

4. It is indispensably necessary to the existence of religion in the family, that there be secured *a proper observance of the Sabbath*, upon the part of all its members.

The two Divine institutions of the family and the Sabbath are, in the appointment of God, closely related to each other. In enjoining a holy rest from toil, each member of the household is distinctly specified, whether parent or child, master or servant. It is to be hallowed by *the family*, as such, with appropriate duties and exercises. Now, when we consider the end for which the family is constituted, we discover the wisdom of this arrangement. For what can be better adapted to promote that end, than the appointment of one day in seven, in which, undisturbed by worldly cares, and with no hour that is not hallowed to sacred purposes, we may convert the house into a little sanctuary, and lead the thoughts and devotions of old and young towards their Creator? Of all the many aids to family religion that exist, none can equal this one. If the six days' work of God was "very good," it scarcely furnished a greater display of his wisdom than his exemplary rest upon the seventh, and his consecrating it, for all time, to his peculiar service.

The opportunities of religious instruction upon that day are evident, and are within the reach of all. No parent can afford to neglect them. The sacred character of the day, the holy stillness, the solemn pause of busy life without and within, the services of God's house, with its reverent throng of worshippers, all combine to render it a season most favourable to the inculcation of Divine truth. Each consecrated hour, as it passes, speaks of God. All nature, left free to utter the voice which the six days of human art and toil had well nigh drowned, speaks of God. The Bible, that third great gift, which links together the Sabbath and the family, and affords the means of fulfilling the end of both, speaks of God and Christ, of duty and comfort, of heaven and hell. Now its truths are heard from the family altar, now from the Sabbath-school, again from the preacher's lips, and yet again in the instructions of the fireside. Who can estimate the tremendous power of a well spent Sabbath over the family, or its value as a means in the hand of the faithful parent? It is above all price, and they know not what they lose, who do not avail themselves, to the utmost, of its advantages.

We are not, however, to regard this as a means which we are at liberty to employ, or dispense with, as pleases us. The obligation to keep holy the Sabbath day rests equally upon all. We owe it to God, as his creatures and subjects, that we not only hallow it as individuals, but also secure its strict observance upon the part of "son" and "daughter," "man-servant" and "maid-servant." We owe it to our children that they be not deprived of their spiritual advantages of the day. This is not only their privilege, but their *right*, which, in the name of Jehovah, they may justly claim at our hands.

The connection between filial piety, and the due observance of that day is set forth in the Divine command, "Ye shall fear every man his mother and his father, and ye shall keep my Sabbaths: I am the Lord." Lev. xix. 3. In fulfilment of this duty, the child should early be impressed with the sacred character of the Lord's day, and the Divine command concerning it, and be trained to a holy awe of every thing that would tend to its violation. These instructions should be illustrated and enforced by example; and the parent should reflect that Sabbath-breaking in himself is a double sin, because encouraging it in those who are so ready to imitate his conduct. Care is indeed to be taken that holy time do not become "a weariness" to the family, but none are therefore warranted in profaning it. It is only necessary that instruction be presented in a form calculated to interest, rather than repel, and pleasure will be mingled with profit, and both old and young may be led to look forward to this as the

"Day of all the week the best;"

and, by the blessing of God, learn to "call the Sabbath a delight, the holy of the Lord, honourable."

As a necessary part of the due observance of this day, children should *early be led by their parents to the sanctuary*, and be required to attend reverently upon its worship. That the act of joining in public worship, when permitted in the providence of God to do so, is essential to the proper observance of the Sabbath, is plain from the command of God in which the two duties are united: "Ye shall keep my Sabbaths and reverence my sanctuary." Lev. xix. 30. A mistake is sometimes made in keeping young children from the house of God, under the impression that they may, by their conduct, disturb others, or annoy the minister. Yet every one who knows the importance of early habits in this respect, had rather submit to the restlessness which is not unnatural in a little child, than have it debarred an attendance upon means of grace. Especially will the right minded pastor be willing to endure a temporary annoyance from the lambs of the flock, rather than have them deprived, year after year, of the privileges of God's house.

It will, however, generally be found that correct habits may be formed without much difficulty; and that they who have learned rightly to deport themselves in the worship of the family, will soon acquire an appropriate demeanour when engaged in that of the sanctuary. It may be objected that young children are incapable of comprehending a discourse addressed to older and more cultivated minds. Be this as it may, much is gained by forming the early *habit* of attending church. There are, however, few preachers of the gospel in its purity and simplicity, a part of whose discourses, at least, are not adapted to the apprehension of childhood. The perceptions of the little one are sometimes as clear as those of many an ignorant, illiterate man or woman who may be found in an ordinary Sabbath congregation. The gospel is, itself, clear and simple, and he who "gives to each a portion in due season," will not forget the "milk for babes."

It is held by some that nothing can be gained by compelling a child to attend church *against its will.* This principle, if carried to its full extent of application, would absolve the parent from all religious duty to his offspring; for what obligation of piety is not more or less against the will of a depraved and sinful creature? This plea, however, is sometimes shown to be fallacious, by the effectual operation of Divine truth upon even unwilling listeners. A pious father asked his refractory son, one Sabbath morning, if he was going to church. The child answered that he was not, pleading at the same time some trivial excuse. "But you shall ride and I will walk," said the father. The child, being resolved not to go, made many objections, which were answered in a similar way; until, no longer able to hide the opposition of his heart, he exclaimed, "I will go, but I will not hear one word." He then went away in a passion. Now mark the result. The Holy Spirit not only caused him to hear with attention, but fastened the truth with such power upon his mind that he was deeply convicted of sin, and was unable to leave the place without assistance. After several days of distress, he found peace in the blood of Christ, and is now a preacher of that gospel which he had so despised, and had determined not to hear.

It will be comparatively in vain that all other good influences are brought to bear upon the minds of our offspring, if this one be withheld. It is *God's own plan* for the furtherance of the end for which the family is ordained, and they who dispense with it must proportionably fail of that end, fall far short of duty, and incur a fearful responsibility. The parent who permits his child to grow up a Sabbath-breaker, is thereby sowing the seeds of future sin and crime, and need not be surprised if they ripen to a fearful harvest. It will rather be matter for wonder if those who are thus reared *do not* come to some unhappy end.

From the mass of convincing testimony to this effect which has been spread before the public, we select that of a gentleman who has had charge, at different times, of more than one hundred thousand prisoners. Having taken special pains to ascertain the causes of their crimes, he declares that he does not recollect a single case of capital offence where the party had not been a

Sabbath-breaker; and that in many cases they assured him that Sabbath-breaking was the *first step* in their downward course. Indeed he says, with reference to prisoners of all classes, "nineteen out of twenty have neglected the Sabbath and other ordinances of religion." A father, whose son was addicted to riding out for pleasure on the Sabbath, was told that if he did not stop it, his son would be ruined. Instead, however, of heeding this advice, he himself would occasionally set the example of such desecration. That son, in after life, was twice entrusted with large amounts of money, of which in each instance he defrauded the owner, and fled. He was apprehended, sent to the State prison, and after years of solitary labour, wrote a letter to his father, recounting his career of crime, and adding, "*That was the effect of breaking the Sabbath when I was a boy.*"

Instances of this kind might be multiplied, but these will suffice. The providence of God unites with his word in attesting our duty upon this subject. We appeal, then, to the parent, as he would be faithful to God and to his offspring, as he would save those whom he tenderly loves from temporal ruin and a worse spiritual destruction, as he would train his family for honour instead of shame, for God instead of Satan, and for heaven instead of hell, to promote among them, by all means in his power, *the strict observance of the holy Sabbath.*

CHAPTER VII.

MEANS, CONTINUED.—PARENTAL PRAYER.

V. It will already have occurred to the Christian parent, that in order to give efficacy to any of the means that have been enumerated, and successfully to promote religion in the family, we must employ the instrumentality of PRAYER.

The promise, "Ask, and it shall be given you; seek, and ye shall find," is susceptible of the widest application. It addresses the burdened sinner as he looks wistfully towards the cross of Christ, and seeks "peace in believing;" it is a word of encouragement to the afflicted or desponding child of God; it is an animating voice to the toiler in the Lord's vineyard, and to him who mourns the desolations of Zion; and it is a command of blessed import to *the parent*, whose "heart's desire" is bid to shape itself in "prayer to God" for the conversion of his offspring. It is as available for others as for ourselves, and is as necessary to the work of training immortal souls for the Divine glory, as it is to our individual salvation. For, notwithstanding all the means placed in our hands, they are *only* means to an end which none but God can accomplish. No degree of fidelity in instruction and discipline, in example and precept, can of itself convert a soul. These are simply the instrumentalities which Divine grace is pleased usually to bless to that end. Everything then depends, after all, upon the blessing of God, and the influences of his Spirit upon the hearts of our offspring. How may these be obtained ? We reply, and the whole tenor of God's word, and the voice of all Christian experience, confirm the truth of the statement, *in answer to prayer*. The parent must carry the case of his children to God, just as he has that of his own soul, and plead for the same grace for them that has blessed him with the joys and hopes of piety. Humbly confessing their depraved and undone condition, and their need of the blood of Christ to save them, he should crave for them the convincing and converting influences of the Spirit, in the faith that they will be granted.

It would seem as if the Christian parent should be the last one to distrust the faithfulness of his covenant God; for the Saviour bids him behold in his own affectionate gratification of his children's wants, an emblem of the *more* kind and loving disposition of his heavenly Father. He asks, " What man is there of you, whom, if his son ask bread, will he give him a stone ? or if he ask a fish, will he give him a serpent ?" And what is the conclusion which the " sons and daughters of the Lord Almighty" are to derive from this ? "If ye, then, *being evil,* know how to give good gifts unto yonr children, how much more shall your Father which is in heaven give good things to them that ask him ?" Matt. vii. 9—11. Now what " good things" can we more reasonably ask than that for which God has made us parents, and entrusted our offspring to us—the enfolding of the precious lambs in the flock of the good Shepherd? Perhaps one reason of our Lord's selecting this illustration in preference to others, was because parents have need of so strong a *faith in prayer.* He would have them conclude that He who is all good, cannot be less ready than they, who are "evil," to grant the reasonable request of his children.

With such an evidence before us of the merciful heart of God, we scarcely need add anything upon the importance of parental prayer. It is enough for us to know that he "heareth prayer," that he encourages our approaches to the mercy-seat, and will not drive away the humble suppliant. The truly Christian parent will not ask, "Is it my duty?" but realizing the blessedness of enlisting the heavenly Father's aid, and bringing Divine influences to bear in securing the eternal well being of his children, will be content to know that it is his *privilege* to pray for them, in hope of a favourable answer.

1. They who would rightly avail themselves of this privilege will pray *in secret* for their children. The retirement of the closet, where no eye but that of Him "who seeth in secret," is upon us, is most favourable to the full and earnest outpouring of the heart to God. There we may breathe forth those desires which words fail wholly to express, and engage with all our powers in the work of intercession for those we love, with no thought of another's criticism to dampen our ardour, or check our importunity. There we may wrestle as Jacob did, until, as princes, we have "power with God," and "prevail." Could the success of many a pious parent be traced to its source, it would no doubt be found that

it is not owing so much to any extraordinary qualifications of nature, as to his earnest closet devotions, and to the grace and wisdom thence derived. He may enter the retired spot with a heart weary and dispirited, and ready to fail under the burden of its responsibilities; but as he waits on the Lord, he renews his strength, and he comes forth nerved and invigorated for new duties and new trials.

The parent, however, is not blessed alone. He cries with Abraham, Let my son, my daughter, "*live before thee!*" and as he implores, upon bended knees, the conversion of his children, his is a power, though invisible, that is superior to that of the world and sin. The sighs, the groans, the tears that choke the whispered utterance of the mother praying for her children, exert an influence greater than the decrees of kings, or the movements of armed hosts, for they rise acceptably to the throne of heaven, and their answer affects the issues of eternity. Thus the "still small voice" is ever stronger than the whirlwind; and in religion, as in the operations of nature, the most effective processes are those that are silent, and unobserved by the eye of man. The prayer of faith, when thus offered, is generally "rewarded openly" in the ingathering of one after another of the family to Christ, and their public, consistent confession of his name.

It also seems appropriate that *special seasons of prayer* should be observed in relation to each member of the family. Allusion has already been made to the duty of consecrating our children to God by a distinct private as well as public act. What can be more proper than, upon such occasions, to wrestle with a peculiar earnestness for their salvation? In dedicating them solemnly and deliberately to the Lord, parental faith stands on its highest vantage ground, and occupies a position which it cannot too diligently improve. Then is a time for pleading the promise of the covenant, and claiming its grace in their behalf, by entreating that they do, indeed, become the Lord's, body and soul, for time and eternity. It is related of the parents of the late Rev. Dr. Finley, that it was their practice, soon after the birth of each of their children, thus to set apart a day for special prayer that it might be an heir to eternal life; and that they had the happiness of seeing their eight children, seven of whom were sons, distinguished by their piety in youth, and growing in grace as their years increased. "Most of them lived to an advanced age, were useful in their spheres, and greatly respected and beloved on account of their Christian character."

Much is also gained, not only by praying for children, but *with them.* Were there no other benefits to be derived from this practice, all will perceive its importance as a means of instructing them in the duty and proper method of prayer. Great as is the value and efficacy of a father's or mother's petitions in their behalf, they should early be taught themselves to pray. This end may be partially secured, by seeing that they offer, each night and morning, some brief, simple prayer which is adapted to childhood's mind. The bearings of this habit upon the subsequent character of the young can hardly be estimated. It is said that John Quincy Adams, during his long and eventful life, never omitted saying, when he retired to rest, that beautiful prayer which his mother had taught him when a child, beginning,

"Now I lay me down to sleep."

In addition, however, to this, it is important that children be accustomed to hear *a parent's voice* pleading their welfare at the throne of grace. In the imitative spirit of childhood, they will then be the more likely to pray for themselves and others; while they will at the same time acquire a better conception of the nature of prayer, by seeing it illustrated and exhibited before their eyes.

And what a powerful evidence is thus afforded of *the intensity of the parental desire for their conversion*, and therefore of its importance to them! Counsels and admonitions may fall upon the ear unheeded, but there is that in the spectacle of a loved mother, wrestling in agony of supplication for their conversion, which few minds can wholly resist. It evinces a depth of solicitude upon her part which is well calculated to lead them to reflection, and to become a means in the hand of God of the early fulfilment of the petitions thus offered. Many a wayward son will confess to an experience something like that of John Newton. He "became a wicked wanderer, forsook friends, and home, and every virtue," but often in his midnight revelry he would fancy that he felt the soft hand of his mother upon his head, pleading with God, as in childhood's hours, to forgive and bless her boy; and that pure memory, clinging to him through many years of wandering, was at length the means blessed to the bringing back of the prodigal, and he became a successful preacher of the gospel.

"*My mother's prayers haunt me like a ghost,*" exclaimed a young sailor who had entered a place of worship, and taken his seat in an obscure corner. It was in the town of his nativity, which he had abandoned many years before, leaving his widowed mother, and the restraints of a religious home, for a career of vice and profligacy. But he had not wholly forgotten the early instructions of that mother, nor the importunity with which she had formerly plead with God for his salvation; it having been her practice often to arise at midnight, and kneeling down in the chamber where her little ones were sleeping, wrestle for them in prayer. That mother was now dead, and the remainder of the family scattered. Returning to his native village, the sailor felt anxious to learn something of his kindred. It was a season of religious revival, and he bent his steps to the church where his mother had been accustomed to worship, thinking there to meet some of her old acquaintances, who could give him the desired information. The sacred spot, the thronging recollections, those scenes of midnight prayer, and, more than all, the felt influence of the Holy Spirit, spoke powerfully to his heart, until, "unable to quench the fire within, or longer to conceal his anguish, he exclaimed vehemently, 'My mother's prayers haunt me like a ghost!'" After several weeks of distressing conviction, he found peace in Christ, and became an exemplary member of the same church with which his mother had been connected. That faithful parent had lived and died without witnessing an answer to her petitions, but she had prayed in earnest faith, and, unknown to her, those midnight supplications had fallen, like successive layers, upon the heart of her child, and there left an impression which no years of subsequent crime and folly could erase.

How important, then, it is that the mother pray *with* her children, and carefully link in with their earliest associations this unmistakable token of her anxiety for their conversion! It will form a powerful and lasting motive to anxiety upon their own part, and may become the seed which, though it lie dormant for many years, will afterwards ripen to fruits of piety and blessedness.

Such exercises, if judiciously conducted, will generally be as delightful as they are profitable to both old and young. Richard Cecil says of his own experience in regard to them, "These seasons were always pleasant to us, and we sometimes looked forward to them with impatience." A pious mother, whose practice it has been to pray with all her children from their infancy, recently assured the writer that her eldest daughter, now upwards of twenty years of age, so delights in maintaining this habit of her childhood, that she still comes night and morning, and offers prayer by her side.

Human learning has industriously accumulated a mass of incontrovertible arguments in favour of Christianity, but among them we do not remember to have met with this, which is, practically, one of the most effective—*parental prayer.* Yet could we take the sceptic to the lonely chamber, whose very walls seem consecrated by the frequent devotions they have echoed, and bid him look upon the mother or father who kneels there, with

11*

the whole soul wrought up to a holy earnestness of desire; could we bid him listen to the pleading tones, the broken words, and gaze upon the solemn, tearful countenance, that yet shines as if it had caught some rays of the light and glory into which the heart was penetrating; and tell him that all this is a scene daily renewed, and that its object is the salvation of a little child, we think his lips would falter, ere they pronounced religion *a delusion.* In the same manner the child will be led unconsciously to confess the Divine power of Christianity, when he sees it so moving the parental heart; and the sound of a mother's voice, engaged in supplication, will tell more effectively in its favour, than volumes of abstruse argumentation.

Were there more of importunate parental prayer, there would be less of scepticism in the world. Let those, then, who would arm the tender mind against the infidelity that so alarmingly prevails, be careful not to withhold this practical refutation of its claims.

Let us not, however, forget the *direct object* of this kind of prayer, in the view of its incidental benefits. Its chief value lies in the fact that it is God's own means for securing the salvation of souls. Even if it make no discernible impression, whether immediate or remote, upon the minds of our offspring, and if we cannot always trace a connection between it as a means and the desired effect, it is still a sacred duty, that is incumbent upon all who sustain the relation of a parent. This is implied in those precepts which bid us train up our children "in the nurture and admonition of the Lord;" for the imposing of any obligation necessarily enjoins the use of the means requisite to its fulfilment. Prayer is an indispensable means to the discharge of parental duty, and therefore is required of every one upon whom that duty rests. Without it, who is equal to the task of moulding immortal minds, and rightly exerting those influences whose results may be unending? Without it, who can so discharge his fearful responsibilities as to remain free from the blood of souls? How, especially, can any one hope for the conversion of his offspring to God, a work that is so peculiarly dependent upon Divine influences, who withholds prayer to that end?

Many and urgent are the *motives* to this duty. The temptations to which the young are subjected, the wants of the church, the pressing claims of the Redeemer's service, the binding character of parental vows, the unerring faithfulness of the Divine promise, and, more than all, the value of their precious, immortal spirits, lying under the curse, unite in demanding that to all other kinds of effort be added this, of fervent, importunate, unceasing prayer.

And many are the *encouragements* to its use. The Bible is full of them. As there can hardly be a more appropriate subject of prayer than this which we have contemplated, so we must regard all the Divine promises to prayer as peculiarly addressed to the faithful parent. It is scarcely necessary to remind the Christian of those words which have so often fallen, like sweetest music, upon his heart, forming the sure warrant of his hope, the undoubted pledge of Jehovah's faithfulness: "Every one that asketh, receiveth, and he that seeketh, findeth." "Ask and ye shall receive, that your joy may be full."

"He will fulfill the desire of them that fear him; he also will hear his cry and save him." "All things whatsoever ye shall ask in prayer, believing, ye shall receive." Such is the testimony of God, and shall we distrust it? Is not that heart as unfilial towards its heavenly Father, as it is unparental towards its offspring, that can, in the face of such assurances, neglect to pray for their conversion?

The testimony of experience is to the same effect. Earnest parental prayer is seldom, if ever, known to be in vain. The history of the Church abounds in confirmation of this truth. Some of the most "burning and shining lights" that ever adorned Christianity have delighted in bearing witness to it, and have left upon record grateful tributes to the efficacy of petitions offered over them in childhood. Out of a large class in one of our Theological Seminaries, it was found upon investigation that *all but two* attributed their conversion to the prayers of pious mothers. Says Dr. Abbott, "A few years ago, some gentlemen who were associated in preparing for the ministry, felt interested in ascertaining what proportion of their number had pious mothers. They were greatly surprised and delighted in finding that out of one hundred and twenty students, *over a hundred* had been borne by a mother's prayers, and directed by a mother's counsels, to the Saviour."

The unwritten experience of multitudes is of the same character. With a uniformity resembling the operation of nature's laws, God is seen to hear and answer the prayers of the parents for their children. Sometimes, indeed, the answer is long delayed, and faith is sorely tried, and hope almost expires; but "Faithful is he that hath promised, who also will do it." We do not indeed affirm that all children who are prayed for will eventually be saved, nor that all kinds of parental prayer will be answered. Upon this subject, as upon every other, there are those who "ask and they receive not, because they ask amiss." The prayer of unbelief, or mere formality, is always inefficacious. Neither can we reasonably expect that he who is grossly unfaithful in the duties of family instruction and government, will prevail in prayer equally with the more faithful parent. It is important that these facts be borne in mind; for there are those who make the alleged inefficacy of this means in some instances a reason for doubting the whole course of the Divine government in reference to it. Such facts as we have related would seem to indicate that it is still true that God *generally* answers earnest parental prayer; and it remains to be proved that every such prayer which is not sooner or later answered, *is not defective in some important particular.* Until this can be shown, we must rest upon the sure word of God, instead of an exceptional human experience, and still maintain that

> " It shan't be said that praying breath
> Was ever spent in vain."

The remark of a Christian friend to whom the mother of Augustine was bewailing the hardened impiety of her son, for whom "she gave herself wholly unto prayer," was founded in a not unwarrantable faith: "It is impossible that a child of so many tears should be lost."

A mother who was daily expecting the return home

of her son who was a sailor, heard with alarm that the vessel in which he sailed had been lost. The next morning her gate turned upon its hinges, the door opened, and her wayward, yet beloved child stood before her. "Mother," said he, as the tears coursed down his sunburnt face, "*I knew you'd pray me home.*" When wrecked, the thought occurred to him, "My mother prays; Christians' prayers are answered; I may be saved." "This reflection, when almost exhausted with fatigue, and ready to give up in despair, gave him fresh strength, and he laboured with renewed courage till the harbour was gained." Thus many a parent, whose children, now tossed upon life's stormy sea, shall yet be saved in answer to their persevering prayers, shall be greeted on the threshold of the heavenly home by the returning wanderers, who, next to the ascription of glory to the Divine Author of salvation, will say, "*Mother, I knew you'd pray me home!*"

2. Besides that prayer which is secret, or offered in privacy with children, it is of great importance that the parent maintain FAMILY PRAYER.

This practice has existed from the earliest ages. Indeed, previous to the visible organization of the church, it was the common and approved method of engaging in Divine worship. The patriarchs were the priests and ministers of the Most High to their families, offering sacrifices, and interceding in their behalf. Abraham, during all his journeyings, appears to have erected in every place a temporary altar, upon which to sacrifice for his numerous household. Gen. xii. 5, 8; xiii. 18, &c. Jacob summoned all his household to join him in acts of

Divine worship. Gen. xxxv. 2, 3, 7. Job had his family altar, upon which, it is probable, he offered sacrifices daily. It is remarkable that in the inspired delineation of his character, particular stress is laid upon his fidelity in this respect, as if it were an indispensable part of true piety. Upon occasions of peculiar temptation to his children, he offered greater sacrifices, and more earnest prayers than usual, saying, "It may be that my sons have sinned." "Thus did Job continually," or as it is rendered in the margin of our Bibles, "all the days." Job i. 5. The resolution of Joshua, "As for me and my house, we will serve the Lord," would seem to indicate that the Jewish leader engaged with all his household in frequent, and probably daily exercises of devotion.

Passing to New Testament history, we find frequent mention of those who served God with all their "house" —(as in the case of Cornelius, Crispus, etc.,)—an expression which certainly favours the idea that they led their families in regular, stated, devotional exercises. For whatever may have been the piety of each individual member of those families, they could hardly be said to have served God in their collective, household capacity, except they engaged in this united recognition of the Divine name, and mingled their prayers and praises.

The early Christians, says Coleman, "were examples of devout piety in their families. There, at the domestic altar, they fed the sacred fire of devotion, which burned in their bosoms with a triumphant, deathless flame. Every master of a family fulfilled within the walls of his own house the office of private pastor, keeping up in it a regular course of reading, prayer, and instruction to all the members of his household. Thus every private house was, in the words of Chrysostom, a church to itself." * These family devotions were always accompanied by the reading of the Scriptures, and generally with sacred songs.

Thus has the importance of domestic worship been recognized by the most eminent Christians of all ages; and it will be found that in proportion as it has been neglected, family religion has descended to a low ebb, and the standard of vital godliness greatly declined. Indeed, how could it be otherwise? Have we any warrant for the belief that God will visit with daily bestowments of grace, those who do not daily acknowledge his Fatherly care, and confess their need of his blessing? However the offering of secret prayer may conduce to individual piety, it is by no means adequate to the great end of *family* religion. The Church that craves a peculiar blessing, meets and prays in its capacity of a church. The State, offering thanks for a year of mercies, brings us together in our character of citizens. In the same manner the Family, whose members are blessed together, and who, collectively, need peculiar mercies, should assemble *as a family, and pray collectively.* Nothing can be more appropriate than for those who are sheltered under one roof, fed from one table, and protected by one Providence, to join in one tribute of gratitude to their common Benefactor. Their wants, too, are the same. Alike do they need grace for filial or parental duty, and

* "Ancient Christianity Exemplified."

strength against temptation. They need the same "daily bread;" and it would seem as if our Saviour had the devotions of *the family* especially in view, when he framed the model prayer which says, "Give *us* this day *our* daily bread." Together, also, do they suffer, and where one requires the consolations of the Comforter, *all* require them. Shall, then, the hearts that bleed in sympathy of grief be denied a common solace at the mercy-seat? If it is impossible for any member of the family to isolate himself from the joys or sorrows of all the rest, why should each remain in a state of separation from the others in this exercise, which adds a zest to the one, and extracts from the other its sharpest sting? It will be seen that if identity of interest and of obligation, of wants and of enjoyments forms any motive to union in worship, there is no social assemblage that has such powerful reasons for praying together as the family.

Prayer is every where recognized as an indispensable part of true religion. It follows from this that in order to the existence of *family* religion there must be *family prayer*. The very heathen have their household gods whom they worship daily. Shall Christianity, then, be the only religion that is debarred from the home and fireside, and confined to the public sanctuary? Indeed, if the fact be once admitted that the family is a sacred, Divine institution, all of whose lesser ends are to be held subordinate to the greater one of glorifying God by training souls for his service, we see not how any can escape the conclusion that it should daily engage in this solemn recognition of Jehovah.

If anything more be needed to establish the importance

of this practice, it is found in the *beneficial effects* which it is calculated to produce upon all who come under its influence. Nothing can contribute more to the peace and order of the household, or so powerfully affect the temper and conduct of both parents and children. As they listen to the words of Scripture, and kneel together before God, the thought may well take possession of every heart, "*The Lord is in this place.*" The sinful thought or action is rendered doubly so by the presence of the family altar; and besides the grace diffused in answer to prayers thus offered, the very recollection of the united morning devotions will often suffice to check the angry word, and banish the thought of unkindness. When, too, at evening, the assembled household gathers once more to ask the Divine forgiveness and protection, the acts of the day pass in review before each mind, its sins are deplored and confessed, and hearts that had perhaps begun to array themselves in opposition to each other, blend sweetly and harmoniously together. The sway of love, however it may have been temporarily interrupted, resumes its sceptre, the kiss of affection follows, and heaven smiles upon the happy, united family, as they securely "abide under the shadow of the Almighty."

Nor must we overlook the momentous bearings of family worship upon the great ends of *instruction and government.* What admirable opportunities are here afforded for inculcating Divine truth, as, morning and evening, it is derived fresh from its fountain head! What treasures of Bible lore may thus, in the course of a single year, be poured into the mind and heart!

The religious impressions of the young are by this means daily renewed, conscience is insensibly being educated and kept active, the power of temptation is weakened, the appeals of religion strengthened, and a hallowed influence exerted which forms an invaluable preparative for, and aid to the service of God, both here and hereafter. In what a sacred aspect, too, does it clothe the head of the family, who officiates as its priest to God in offering the morning and evening sacrifice! The little group, whose devotions he is accustomed to lead, look up to him with esteem and reverence, and almost intuitively "honour" that father or that mother, who is the daily representative of God to them, and of them to God.

Now what family can afford to dispense with this delightful and profitable means of grace? What conceivable circumstances can warrant any parent in depriving his children of such manifest advantages? We are forced to the conclusion that such as do habitually neglect it are thereby incurring positive guilt and misery. We know of no encouragement for them to hope for their children's conversion. Nay, more than this, they are not only liable to be unblessed, but exposed to the peculiar curse of Him whom they so dishonour. "Pour out thy fury," says a prophet, "upon the heathen that know thee not, and *upon the families that call not upon thy name!*" Jer. x. 25. They cannot justly expect to be prospered, either temporally or spiritually, who withhold this reasonable acknowledgment of God's providence and grace. Upon the other hand, God honours those who thus honour him.

"His mercy visits every house
That pays its night and morning vows."

The consciousness of the Divine presence, with which this practice renders us familiar, sweetens every joy, and lightens every burden. It sanctifies our cares, adds a zest to the season of prosperity, and when adversity overtakes us, imparts a happy sense of repose in the pavilion of the Almighty. It is to the family what the pillar of cloud and fire was to the Israelites: in the morning a guide to point out the day's march through the wilderness, and at evening a token of Divine protection and defence. Happy is the household, and likely to be secure in all their journeyings towards "the place of which the Lord said, I will give it thee," whose first glance at dawn of day, and last look through the shadows of the night, is thus earnestly and unitedly bent towards the Shekinah that dwells upon the mercy-seat.

Perhaps little need be added as to the proper *method* of conducting the worship of the family. A selection from the Scriptures should always be read, in connection with which, brief comments, or appropriate meditations selected from the pages of religious literature, are sometimes beneficial. The practice of reading a chapter from the Bible in rotation, each person repeating one or two verses in his turn, often adds to the interest, and serves to retain attention upon the part of the young. The prayer should be simple, appropriate, and as comprehensive as is consistent with a due regard to brevity. The addition of sacred praise assists materially in promoting cheerful devotion. Indeed, no worship of God can be deemed complete, from which this is omitted.

The remarks of the Rev. Dr. J. W. Alexander upon this subject are forcible and true.* "We ask attention to the assertion that there is no argument for sacred music in the church, which does not hold equally good in the family. Though this part of the service has fallen out of the practice of many households, and (strangely enough) extensively in those regions where scientific music has been most boastfully cultivated, the judgment of our church on this subject is explicit. 'It is the duty of Christians to praise God, by singing psalms or hymns, publicly, in the church, *as also privately, in the family*.'" † Care is to be taken that these exercises be not so protracted as to produce weariness, nor so brief and hasty as to conflict with the solemnity that the occasion demands.

The devotions should be led by the father, or in his absence, or in a family that is widowed and fatherless, by the mother. Those parents who, from diffidence or inexperience, cannot bring themselves to pray aloud before the family, had better use in the beginning some of the admirable forms of prayer that are prepared for the purpose, rather than wholly omit so sacred a duty. These helps, however, ought not to be so much relied upon as to prevent suitable efforts towards acquiring the habit of praying *extempore*. It is generally found to be more profitable to pray from a full heart, in language that naturally occurs to us, than habitually to make even the most finished and appropriate of human compositions the vehicle of our addresses to the throne of grace.

* Thoughts on Family Worship.

† Directory for Worship. chap. iv. § 1.

As an important part of domestic worship, and an appropriate exercise of family religion, may be added the duty of *asking the Divine blessing at table.* This is only a just and proper recognition of our dependence upon God; and it savours strongly of ingratitude to partake of the bounties of his providence without such an acknowledgment of their kind Giver. The sorrowful inquiry of the little boy, upon an occasion when this duty was omitted, "Is there no God to-day, father?" might properly be put to every one who partakes of a meal which the Divine hand has spread, with no word of petition or thanksgiving to God. It was the practice of the early Christians not only to offer prayer before meals, but to recite portions of Scripture, and sing praise to God, and at their close to return thanks for the mercies they had enjoyed. While there may be no necessity of such protracted exercises, the Christian scarcely needs to be reminded that God should be honoured in the enjoyment of his blessings. The influence of this exercise upon the family is highly beneficial, connecting, as it does, the Giver with the gifts, and affording a practical fulfilment of the injunction, "Whether ye eat, or drink, or whatever ye do, do all to the glory of God."

CHAPTER VIII.

THE RELATION OF THE FAMILY TO THE CHURCH.

Every part of the Divine government is characterized by a beautiful harmony of adaptation. An endless series of connections and dependencies is found to exist both in the domain of providence and grace, linking all things together as parts of that grand whole which lies spread out under the eye of God. In successive gradations the physical ministers to the moral, and the temporal to the eternal. Thus the earth was adapted, in the Divine wisdom, to the man; the body, formed from the dust, was prepared for the soul that should inhabit it; the first human pair was the foundation of the family; and the family, in like manner, was the necessary intermediate step towards the organization of *the church.*

The connection that exists between these two institutions, and the relations that they sustain to each other are plain to every reflecting mind. The one is, in a manner, the basis of the other, not only in a natural point of view, as furnishing the material of which it is composed, but also morally, as endowed by God with similar features, and ordained for a like end. While differing in many respects, they yet resemble each other in their main object, which is the culture and development of man's higher, spiritual nature, and in their means and appliances, which consist, in both cases, in instruction, discipline, and worship. These resemblances would seem to indicate that they are, in the government of God their Author, closely related, and possessed of important bearings the one upon the other.

That such is the case may also be inferred *from the nature of that Divine covenant with Abraham which formed*, as we have seen, *the organization of the visible Church.* Previously to that time, sacrifices had been offered, and worship rendered, *by families*, the heads of which officiated as priests for all the household. For many centuries, therefore, the pious family approached the nearest of any existing institution to the idea of the visible Church. When it pleased God to found a church, with its initiating seal, and covenant of promise, he proceeded upon this principle, which had become so firmly established, and organized *a single family* as the nucleus about which were to be gathered the multitudes of his professed people in all ages. Nor did he stop here; but, as if for ever to impress the truth of the connection between the one and the other, he incorporated into the constitution of his church the promise: "I will establish my covenant between me and thee, *and thy seed after thee*, in their generations, to be a God to thee and to thy seed after thee;" Gen. xvii. 7; and again, "In thee shall *all the families* of the earth be blessed."

We are indeed taught by the apostle that they who

are Christ's, are "Abraham's seed, and heirs according to the promise;" yet that the sense of this covenant was not wholly spiritual, is proved by the fact that the literal seed of the patriarch did, for so many generations, constitute the body of God's people upon earth. The covenant, then, which lies at the foundation of the visible church, was not formed with Abraham and other believers, simply as individuals, but also as *heads of families.* "The promise," said Peter, "is to you and your children." It is true that many, whose parents had no interest in this promise, do yet become converted; as also, upon the other hand, not all children who are born within the pale of the church, maintain their birthright privilege by a consistent Christian profession. Still the fact holds good that the church, in its true idea, is an aggregate and succession of pious families, chosen out of the world as the depositary of the oracles and ordinances of religion, and in turn transmitting them to their descendants.

This relation of the family to the church is expressly declared by God *in the ordinances of circumcision and baptism,* the administration of which to children is founded, as we have seen, upon the doctrine of infant church membership as enunciated in the Abrahamic covenant. The head of the family, under the Old Testament dispensation, was solemnly bound to circumcise, not only each one of his offspring, but also his servants; thus bringing the entire household into a state of connection with the visible church. So when a proselyte from a heathen nation embraced Judaism, he did not, if a parent, enter into covenant alone, but took his children with him and they all were circumcised *as a family.* This precious doctrine was not changed by the change of its seal, nor were the rights and privileges of the children of believers in any way abridged by our Saviour. When the parent embraced the Christian faith, and was admitted to the church by baptism, the household came with him. Thus Lydia was baptized, "and her household." The Philippian jailer "was baptized, and all his." Crispus "believed on the Lord with all his house." Paul makes mention of having baptized "the household of Stephanas." See Acts xvi. 15, 33; xvii. 8; 1 Cor. i. 16.

This relationship of the families of believers to the church has been recognized by the great body of believers from the days of the apostles to the present time. We discover frequent mention of it in the writings of the fathers, and in the standards of the Reformed churches. The French Confession of Faith (A. D. 1539) declares that baptism is to be administered "to infants born of holy parents;" the Belgic, or Reformed Dutch, (A. D. 1566,) "to the children of the faithful;" the Confession of Helvetia, (A. D. 1636,) "to such as are born of the people of God." The Confession of Faith of the Presbyterian Church says, that "the infants of one or both believing parents are to be baptized;" and the Larger Catechism, carrying this doctrine to its legitimate conclusion, defines the visible church as "a society made up of all such as, in all ages and places of the world, do profess the true religion, *and of their children.*" (Ques. 62.) As defined in the Form of Government, (Chap. ii. § 2,) "The universal church consists of all those persons, in every nation, *together with their children*, who make profession of the holy religion of Christ, and of submission to his laws."

Such, then, is the relation of the families of believers to the church. Ordained by God at its first organization, it yet remains a token of the Divine goodness and wisdom, a comfort to God's people, and a blessing to the Redeemer's kingdom. Parental faith still claims and pleads the promise, "I will be a God to thee and to thy seed after thee," and the church delights in acknowledging the lambs of the flock as her own, by receiving them within her fold, and pledging to them her prayers and counsels. What an admirable provision is this for the mutual good of these kindred institutions! Being thus closely linked together, the Christian family is made the means of preparing souls for Christ's service in the church, and of furnishing those children who shall be instead of the fathers, in the successive generations of God's people; while the church pays back an abundant recompense into the bosom of the family, by coöperating in its work of training young souls for God and heaven. In the Divine economy, each is, when fulfilling its part, a help-meet for the other. Neither is complete in itself, but they form, unitedly, a grand and perfect scheme, exactly adapted to the furthering of the end which they alike have in view. The one takes the infant in its dawning reason, and consecrates to holy ends the only influences that can then be brought to bear upon it. Soon the other steps in with its strengthening and confirming means of grace. For a season they labour unitedly, each taking a hand of the tender child, and leading him in paths of piety—each bearing a part in the task of rearing it in the nurture and admonition of the Lord—until, in years of maturity, the ties of the one family being perhaps dissevered, and, by the blessing of God, its end having been accomplished, the other has taken its place, and carries on its work. The instruction and government begun at a mother's knee, is thus maintained to the latest hours of life. The truths that fell on the quick ear of infancy in the little domestic sanctuary, still address the ear of age in the house of God; and the good seed that parental hands had planted with prayers and tears, is fostered and cultivated by the church, until it becomes a tree, all laden with fruits of piety. Thus the work goes on, until the ripened saint is gathered to that society where family and church, having fulfilled their appointed task, mingle for ever into one, in the upper home and sanctuary, "not made with hands, eternal in the heavens."

Like every other relation, this one implies *certain corresponding duties.* Some of these have already been adverted to, such as the administration of baptism to all infants of believers, and the instruction and discipline of the family. In addition, however, to these, are *the peculiar duties of the church* towards those who are thus born within its pale. That the church owes certain specific obligations to all its members, is a fact which it requires no argument to prove. As, then, the children of professed believers are, by virtue of its constitution, its members, it is only necessary to ask, What are the peculiar rights and privileges to which their membership entitles them? Upon this subject many loose and erroneous views prevail, which it shall be our aim, as far as possible, to correct. In some churches, indeed, there is scarcely any recognition of duty towards baptized children; and the anomaly is presented, (of which the opponents of pædobaptism have readily availed themselves), of an acknowledged membership that practically entitles to no privileges, and imposes no obligations. Perhaps one great failure upon the part of the church at the present day is in this direction. We therefore ask every Christian who coincides in the premises that have just been laid down, attentively to consider the necessary conclusions to which they lead.

The duties of the church in this particular may be included under the general heads of INSTRUCTION, DISCIPLINE, AND PRAYER.

1. *Instruction.* None will contend that the children of believers do not need to be taught in Divine things at least equally with those who are older, nor that it is not the church's duty to instruct her members. Why then should they be denied this privilege who, by reason of their tender age, so peculiarly require it? The voice of Jesus to the repentant Peter is addressed to the church at large, "Lovest thou me?" "*Feed my lambs!*" In these words our Lord claims a close and endearing relationship to the children of the church. He calls them *his* "lambs;" and his they are by a triple tie—that of creation, preservation, and more than all in their character of "the seed of the blessed of the Lord." This "threefold cord," that "is not quickly broken," binds the multitudes of the church's offspring to the throne and the heart of Jesus; and he justly appeals to our love

13

for him as a sufficient motive for feeding them with the food which he has himself provided. The lambs of the flock have, then, a heaven-derived claim upon the church for spiritual nurture, and we cannot, without violating our most solemn obligations, withhold it from them.

This duty is also demanded by the very instinct of *self-preservation*. The children of the church are, in an eminent degree, the *hope* of the church. God can, indeed, perpetuate his kingdom upon earth without them. As John the Baptist declared to the boastful Pharisees, he "is able of these stones to raise up children to Abraham." Yet experience attests that the great body of believers in all ages are those born within the covenant, and that it is to our baptized offspring that we are chiefly to look for our probable successors in the faith. How important, then, the duty of early indoctrinating them in Divine truth, of teaching them "the form of sound words," and taking all necessary pains towards the rearing of a generation of *intelligent* as well as earnest Christians! To neglect this duty, is to leave the church open to every form of error, and to commit its dearest interests to those who will be but ill qualified to maintain and defend them. We believe it will be found that in proportion as this obligation has been recognized and faithfully discharged, religion has been preserved in its purity, while its disuse has ever been one of the most fruitful sources of heresy and schism. We are greatly indebted, under God, to the fidelity of our forefathers in this respect, for the present prevalence of evangelical views and doctrines; and upon the church's continued discharge, or evasion of this duty, will equally depend the orthodoxy of the coming generation. Do we not therefore owe it to ourselves and our posterity, to the present and to the future, that we diligently feed Christ's lambs?

The church at large has always acknowledged the necessity of instructing her baptized children. The primitive Christians regarded them as justly entitled to their earnest solicitude, and faithful nurture in Divine things. Augustine says, "Children were presented to baptism, not so much by those in whose hands they were brought, (though by them too, if they were good and faithful men,) as by the whole society of saints. *The whole church was their mother.*" Nor did they evade the responsibilities of this so called maternal relation. Besides the instructions of the home, in which the early Christians were remarkably faithful, the baptized children, "in all places where it was practicable, had, from the very commencement of the Christian church, the opportunity of attending *catechetic schools.*" The celebrated school of Alexandria, which is supposed to have been founded by Mark the Evangelist, was of this character, and embraced in its instructions both Divine and human learning. In this school, Eusebius informs us, Clemens Alexandrinus and Origen taught. "Similar schools existed in Rome, Cesarea, Antioch, Ephesus, and other places." They were generally "kept in churches, where they were erected, or in buildings adjoining to the church; which is evident," says Bingham, "from the observation which Socrates makes upon the education of Julian the Apostate, that in his youth he frequented the church where, in those days, the schools were kept." In the fourth century, Gregory " set up schools in every city, and masters over them by the king's command, to teach the Armenian children to read the Bible."

As the corruptions of Popery increased, Christian education was more generally neglected; although we read of cathedral schools being maintained in the seventh, eighth, and ninth centuries. These, however, as might be supposed, were attended with but slight success in either a religious or literary point of view. Indeed the efforts of the papacy were concentrated *against* the faithful instruction of the young; and while permitting them but a meagre education in the most ordinary branches of human learning, it deliberately withheld from them the sacred Scriptures, substituting in their place the most childish fables and traditions. As the heathen emperor Julian attempted to banish the children of Christians from the schools of learning, " lest they should be qualified to argue with the gentile dialecticians," so Pope Paul II., in his efforts to engraft paganism upon a nominal Christianity, declared, "It is sufficient for the sons of Christians that they be taught to read and write."

When the Reformation of the sixteenth century burst upon the world, its adherents realized the importance of a return to the primitive practice in this respect, and thereby availed themselves of a most invaluable method of extending the knowledge and influence of the truth. Thus, in the discipline of the Reformed Churches of France, it was enjoined, "1. That the churches shall do their utmost to endeavour to erect schools, and to take care of the instruction of her youth. 2. Regents and masters of schools shall subscribe the confession of faith, and church discipline, and the towns and churches shall not admit any one into this office without the consent of the consistory of that place." In the same book of discipline, "Fathers and mothers are directed to be exhorted to be very careful of their children's education, who are the seed plat, and promising hopes of God's church. And therefore such as send them to school to be taught by priests, monks, jesuits, and nuns, shall be prosecuted with all church censures."

The Reformed Church of Holland was also extremely solicitous for the religious instruction of the young under proper ecclesiastical auspices; providing not only institutions of higher grade for the education of the ministry, but also the parochial school for children. The Synod of Dort, (A. D. 1619,) a convention in which were represented not only the Dutch, but every other Reformed Church upon the continent, together with the Established Church of North Britain, decreed as follows: "In order that the Christian youth may be diligently instructed in the principles of religion, and be trained in piety, three modes of catechizing should be employed. I. In the house, by parents. II. In the schools by school-masters. III. In the churches by ministers, elders, and catechists especially appointed for the purpose. That these may diligently employ their trust, they shall be requested to promote by their authority so sacred and necessary a work; and all who have the oversight of churches and schools shall be required to pay especial attention to this matter." Under the different heads above noted, we read that the office of parents is, "diligently to instruct their children and their whole household in the principles of the Christian religion;" "to prepare them for being catechized in the schools, and, by attendance on them, to encourage them, and promote their edification;" and that "parents who profess religion, and are negligent in this work, shall be admonished by the ministers, and if the occasion requires, they shall be censured by the consistory, that they may be brought to the discharge of their duty." "Schools, in which the young shall be properly instructed in the principles of Christian doctrine," were to be established, "not only in cities, but also in towns and country places." None were to be employed as teachers but "such as are members of the church, having certificates of an upright faith, and pious life, and of being well versed in the truths of the Catechism." Ministers, and, if necessary, elders, were required to "visit all the schools, private as well as public, frequently."

The Presbyterian Church of Scotland, from her earliest history, established parochial schools, which were under the direct inspection of her judicatories. In the reign of James VI., "none were admitted to instruct the youth, but such as should be tried by the visitors of the Kirk." The General Assembly of 1638 "directed the several presbyteries to settle schools in every landward parish, and provide men able for the teaching of youth." By an act of the Assembly, 1642, a grammar school was erected in every presbytery, seat, and burg. The Assembly of 1700 enjoined it upon all presbyteries "to take special, particular, and exact notice of all schoolmasters, governors, and pedagogues of youth, within their respective bounds, and oblige them to subscribe the

Confession of Faith, and in case of continued negligence, (after admonition,) error, or immorality, 'or not being careful to educate those under their charge in the Protestant Reformed religion,' points out the mode in which they are to be punished."*

Such is the testimony of the church in past ages. It has ever loved to recognize and act upon the fact of its relationship to the family, and has felt itself solemnly bound to the fulfilment of the duties which that relationship imposes. Nor has the church of the present day proved recreant to her ancestral faith and doctrine, however derelict she may have become in practice.

In the Form of Government of the Presbyterian Church, (Book II. Chap. i. § 6,) it is affirmed, "*All baptized persons are members of the church, are under its care, and subject to its government and discipline.*" The Constitution of the Reformed Dutch Church employs the same language, (Chap. iv. Art. 1. Sec. 3.) Now what is meant by the "care," and "government and discipline" here so plainly set forth, if not that the baptized child as well as the adult is to be faithfully watched over, and admonished in those things that pertain to ecclesiastical oversight, namely, in everything affecting its spiritual and immortal interests? Is not the truth here clearly enunciated that from early infancy, on through the intermediate stages of life, "*all* baptized persons" are to be instructed in the doctrines of religion, and

* See "Duty of the Church in the Instruction and Discipline of her baptized children," (Presb. Board of Publication,) in which may be found more extended extracts from the standards of the Reformed Churches upon this subject.

generally influenced for their good in the use of whatever means the church can legitimately employ? This will, we think, be admitted by all. The only remaining question, then, is, How shall the church best exercise this "care" which she acknowledges to be due from her to her youthful charge?

She should evidently, first of all, *see to it that religious instruction be faithfully maintained in all her households.* We have already considered at length parental duty in this respect, and have seen that it is founded upon the nature and design of the family constitution. We may add, in this connection, that the same obligation flows from the relation of *the church* to her baptized children. It is only through the medium of the parent that she can act upon the mind of early childhood, and it is plainly her duty to use every endeavour that her infant members be correctly instructed in Divine truth. To this end, they who have the spiritual oversight of professing Christians, may well feel themselves bound to insist upon the *early* religious education of the lambs of the flock. Ministers should present this duty from the pulpit with frequency and earnestness, and, with their elders, make it the subject of inquiry and appropriate exhortation in their pastoral visits among the people. The truth ought to be impressed upon every mind that they are guilty of culpable neglect and inconsistency, who suffer the children of the church to grow up under their eyes in a state of spiritual destitution.

"We account ourselves bound," says Hill, in his "Institutes," "to exercise a continued inspection over the Christian education of those who have been baptized, *that, as far as our authority and exertions can be of any avail, parents may not neglect to fulfil their vows.*" The family is, in a manner, the repository of the church, the guardian, to whose sole care she for a season assigns these her precious, immortal trusts. In correspondence with this fact, the position of the Christian parent is one of double responsibility, for he is not only accountable to God, but also to the church, for his influence upon the minds of his offspring.

The church, however, has a responsibility in this matter *which she cannot consistently transfer to others.* There are years in the career of the child or youth, when she may appropriately claim an important part in his moral training—those years between infancy and maturity, in which the mind is peculiarly susceptible, and in a state to be moulded for eternity. How, then, shall her influences be effectively put forth?

Of course the only fountain of truth, whether for the youthful or adult mind, is *the word of God.* Whatever other means be employed, they are only the different channels through which this living water may be conveyed to them. The church, then, through her appointed instructors, should lavishly dispense to her children the pure doctrines and words of the Old and New Testament Scriptures. This may be done through the Sabbath-school, provided that it be under the immediate supervision of the church officers, and that its instructors be qualified, by their sanctified intelligence, for so important a task.

The experience of the past has proved that there is also great moral power in the right use of *catechetical instruc-*

tion. Valuable helps to this duty are at hand, which are the mature fruits of much collective wisdom and patient effort, and which have proved themselves admirably adapted to this work. They have been employed by generations of God's people with signal success, and it would be difficult to exaggerate their influence in the preservation of sound doctrine. They have been approved by our church judicatories, and are placed in our hands as important aids to the inculcation of Bible truth in its order and symmetry. Next to the Scriptures, for which they were never designed to be a substitute, but to which they are a most important auxiliary, they should be faithfully and diligently employed, and should occupy a prominent place in the church's educational means and appliances. In the early history of the church, great care was taken that not only the catechists, who were judiciously selected and appointed for this office, but also pastors, should exercise a close supervision over this part of religious instruction, explaining and applying the truths thus learned, and making the catechism an important link of intercourse between them and the young of their flocks. It is to be regretted that there has been so wide a departure from this practice of our forefathers. To this day the Church of Scotland adheres to her time-honoured custom of thorough catechetical instruction, under the supervision of the proper authorities, and as the result of such fidelity, her name has become synonymous throughout Christendom with sound doctrine, and pure, evangelical religion.

As a valuable means of discharging her acknowledged duty to her children, the church has maintained, from her earliest history, *Parochial Schools*—so called from being under the control and management of the church or parish. In these were employed teachers competent to instruct in all the ordinary branches of school education, and at the same time qualified by their piety and familiarity with Christian doctrine, to teach the Bible and Catechism. By means of these institutions, the young are kept under the eye of the church, during that interesting period which, of all others, is perhaps the most important in the formation of mental and moral habits, yet which is too frequently left to the direction and oversight of the world. Can it be questioned that the church ought to make some provision for these school days, as well as for those of the college, and that duty to her baptized children demands that religion be made to enter into and form part of their *daily* education? Valuable as are the instructions of the Sabbath-school or Bible-class, they are apt to be overwhelmed and forgotten, if those of the week are marked by the absence of religion.

We hear much of a class of professors who are called "Sabbath Christians," or who carry not their piety with them into the intervening round of weekly duties. May we not well fear lest the child or youth who is deprived of daily religious instruction, if he becomes a Christian at all, will be one of that character? Let it also be borne in mind that no studies are so important as those that relate to men's immortal interests, and it will be seen that these should run parallel with, or rather be kept in advance of every other study. That education is incomplete in its most important particular, which develops the intellectual part of our nature in a state of separation from the moral and spiritual. And how are the two to be effectively combined, if not through the instrumentality of *the church?*

It is matter for congratulation that Christians of the present day are beginning to realize these truths, and in some degree to act upon them. The parochial school system is no longer an experiment in our country, but in many places is working out, by the Divine blessing, happy results for the church and the world. Where these, for any reason, are not established, other methods can be adopted for infusing a marked religious element into the schools that are frequented by the children of believing parents. It may be added in this connection that Protestants should never remit their efforts towards retaining in our common schools the reading, and, if possible, the study of the Bible. Many "baptized persons" avail themselves of the munificent provision afforded by the State for their education; and we owe it to them, to the church at large, and to our country, earnestly to maintain a general, comprehensive system of free instruction which shall not omit this most important feature.

So far as regards the higher institutions of learning, the church has made many and powerful advances in the right direction. Whatever difference of opinion may exist upon the subject of parochial schools, it is generally conceded that *colleges* ought to be under immediate ecclesiastical supervision. The years of student life, marked as they are by the absence of home restraints, and parental inspection and authority, may well be watched over by the church with a peculiar solicitude. To that end, it seems important that none be employed as instructors who are not members of the church, and whose example is not clearly and unmistakably in favour of vital godliness. Nor should parents permit their children to enter seminaries of learning that are not thus characterized. The highest degree of mental cultivation, if unsanctified by religion, has been compared to the "putting a drawn sword in the hands of a madman," and is perhaps as likely to prove an injury as a benefit.

Not to dwell further upon this subject, the church ought plainly to regard herself as the proper instructor of "all baptized persons" from the earliest dawn of reason to old age, allowing no period of life to elapse without suitable provision for their wants as moral beings. Were this acknowledged truth to be practically and universally acted upon, it would unquestionably be attended with glorious results. Then we might be spared, in a great degree, the too common spectacle of the children denying the faith of their fathers; a powerful bulwark would be erected against the inroads of error; pure evangelical doctrine would pervade the minds of the rising generation, and bring forth its appropriate fruits; and the church, strengthened by the intelligent piety of her members, would find it more emphatically true than ever before, that "The gates of hell shall not prevail against her."

This active, inquiring age is prolific of every form of heresy. Old systems of error that were supposed to have fled with the vanishing of the dark ages, are again lifting up their heads, and he needs to be thoroughly indoctrinated in "the truth as it is in Jesus," who would avoid being led by them into the paths of death. In imposing the duty of religious instruction, God has placed in the hands of his church a powerful weapon with which to ward off, and finally to conquer this swarming host. Let it be neglected, and none can foretell the disastrous consequences that may be entailed upon posterity. Let it be rightly improved, and our sons, and our sons' sons, as they walk in the steadfast path of righteousness, shall rise up and call us blessed.

2. Besides the duty that we have just considered, the church owes to her youthful members that of *government and discipline.*

The proper method of discharging this obligation towards adult communicants has long been settled. Not so, however, in regard to those who are children. It has been maintained by some that they ought not only to be admonished, when their conduct renders it necessary, but also, as members of the church, to be held subject to suspension and excommunication. This view is founded upon the declaration contained in the Form of Government, (Book II. chap. i. § 6,) that baptized persons, "when they have arrived at years of discretion, are bound to perform all the duties of church members." The practice of the Jewish church is quoted as favouring this interpretation. At the age of thirteen, as the Jewish doctors inform us, "the circumcised children became 'sons of the commandment,' and were bound to perform the duties of adult members," among which was the eating of the passover. Every one who did not observe this feast was commanded to be "cut off from among his people." Num. ix. 13. Both the Jewish and primitive Christian churches inflicted corporeal punishment upon juvenile offenders. This, however, is now regarded by all as opposed to the mild spirit of Christianity.

This whole subject is ably discussed in the report of a committee appointed by the General Assembly of 1811, to answer the following overture from the Synod of Kentucky:—"What steps should the church take with baptized youth, not in communion, but arrived at the age of maturity, should such youth prove disorderly or contumacious?" This learned and interesting document maintained that baptized children, who have reached the years of discretion, and yet fail to "perform all the duties of church members," ought to be subjected to the extremest discipline of the church, should milder measures prove inefficacious. The General Assembly, having made this report the subject of discussion in several of its subsequent sessions, at length discharged the committee, and the subject was indefinitely postponed. "The Assembly," says the preface to this report, "preferred to leave the matter as it stood in the standards of the church, without expressing any opinion."

It will, we think, be generally conceded that the church should, at least, exercise a degree of *watchfulness* over her baptized children, and manifest towards them a tender care and interest. Whether enforcing strict discipline or not, she may surround them with proper Christian restraints, and impress upon their minds their duty of reverencing her authority, obeying her counsels, and fulfilling their vows as her members. The church may also appropriately take cognizance of those customs and practices of society which are calculated to injure the morals of her baptized children, and, as their spiritual guardian, may denounce prevailing sins. Whatever be the method deemed best for the purpose, ought not the principle to be generally made known and practically acted upon, that her children *are peculiarly under her care and oversight, and entitled to her special supervision ?*

3. It is further implied in the relation which we are considering, *that the church pray for her children and youth.* Our remarks upon the subject of parental prayer will apply here; for the church is, in a certain sense, as Augustine has said, the *mother* of all who are born within her pale. It will be seen that, if she is bound to seek and promote their piety, she is by that very fact obliged to use this most effective of all means to that end. She owes it both to herself and them, that she employ her interest at the mercy-seat in their behalf. They are among the most hopeful subjects of prayer. The very existence of the visible church is a standing testimony to the faithfulness of their covenant God, and a warrant for our firmest confidence. To withhold prayer for them not only evinces ingratitude, but argues a misapprehension of the whole character and object of the church upon earth, and of the promise upon which it rests. In view of the terms of the covenant, does it not seem as if there were none who could more justly claim an interest in our petitions?

Shall, then, every other class of human beings be remembered in the devotions of the sanctuary, and the dear children of the covenant alone be forgotten? Shall we embrace in our outstretched arms of faith the wretched and the outcast, the blasphemer and the idolater, and overlook those whom God has placed so peculiarly under our influence, and who are the hope of the church and the world? No; let them rather be made the subjects of a *special* importunity. Let the secret prayers of the parent be strengthened by the united supplications of the church at large. In the house of God, in the social meeting, at the family altar, in short, wherever the people of God assemble, let them engage with earnestness in this work. What thought can be more delightful to the Christian parent, than that the little one who is given to God in baptism, possesses, from that hour, an interest in all the prayers of all the church, and that from every land there are constantly going up earnest supplications for God's blessing upon it!

Such should be the case; for what is the church but one great family, made up of multitudes of lesser ones, who are united under one head, Jesus Christ,—a family which, like others, has its little children who possess an equal claim upon her prayerful attention? We may multiply other instrumentalities, but without this one they will be comparatively valueless. As one may plant a garden ever so thickly with good seed, but much of it will be wasted if it be not watered, so the most faithful instruction in Divine truth will fail of its end, if the Holy Spirit do not accompany it to the heart; and how shall his fostering influences be secured, but in answer to prayer?

Especially, let the church remember in her supplications her *schools and colleges.* To pray for them, is, in effect, to pray for every other interest of Christianity.

For the college is the source of vast influences for good or evil. It contains those who are hereafter to stand as watchmen upon Zion's walls, and adorn other exalted spheres of life with the graces of piety, or else, who are to pervert their learning to the prejudice of true religion, and wield a tremendous power for evil. How fervently, then, should we implore the Divine blessing upon these fountains, that, being purified by grace, their ten thousand streams may diffuse moral life, and health, and beauty in their course! As an illustration of the stupendous benefits which may be conferred upon the church and the world by our faithfulness in this respect, we quote the following from Professor Tyler's Prize Essay on Prayer for Colleges:—"It has been estimated that one revival of religion, which took place in Yale College, under the presidency of Dr. Dwight, raised up ministers who were instrumental in the conversion of fifty thousand souls in one generation."

This duty might be urged upon the ground of the church's own needs, and of the necessity there is of a large increase in the ranks of the ministry; and also in view of the pressing wants of the missionary cause in this day of rapid providential openings to the truth; but it is perhaps sufficient to commend it as growing out of *the relation of the church to her families.* The college is a part of the great system of instruction furnished by the church to her baptized children; and the Christian parent, whose son is within its walls, has a just claim upon her prayers in his behalf, that his talents may be consecrated, as were his body and soul in infancy, to the Lord's service.

Christians have, of late years, peculiarly felt their responsibility in this respect. About the year 1820 was established the concert of prayer for colleges, which was observed at first every Sabbath morning, but finally appointed for the last Thursday of February, in every year, at which time it is now generally held. As might have been expected, a marked blessing has followed these united supplications of the church. It has been estimated that during the first fifteen years of its observance, "fifteen hundred students were made the hopeful subjects of grace, in thirty-six different colleges." Frequent revivals of religion have occurred at about the time set apart for this purpose, and, indeed, in one of the colleges a powerful outpouring of the Holy Spirit took place upon the very day of the concert. It is also an interesting circumstance, and one showing the Divine recognition of the church's relation to the family, that in most of these revivals a large proportion of converts were "children of the covenant." In the Essay of Professor Tyler, already alluded to, statistics are given, which show that out of one hundred and fifty-five young men who were converted in three successive revivals in one college, *there were but eighteen who had not been baptized in infancy*. These facts are significant. They are well calculated to incite parents to the consecration of their offspring to God, and at the same time furnish powerful encouragement to the church to pray for their conversion.

Such are some of the chief duties involved in the relationship of the family to the church. They are imposed by the great Author of these institutions, and cannot be neglected by either without mutual detriment. The family that would fulfil the end of its appointment should realize its obligation, not only to bring its children within the pale of the visible church, but also to coöperate with her, as its most important ally in the work of rearing them for God. The church, upon the other hand, should ever promote the interests of the family by meeting, as far as is practicable, its spiritual wants, and inciting to parental fidelity. While prosecuting with energy her aggressive movements upon the world without, let her not forget to provide liberally for those of her own household. She is not so straitened in her means and appliances that in order to the doing of the one, she need leave the other undone. More than this, every effort that is put forth in behalf of her own children will tell powerfully upon all her benevolent instrumentalities, whether at home or abroad. For it is to them that she must mainly look for filling the ranks of her labourers, and carrying the gospel to the destitute. May we not, then, attribute to a failure in this particular, the fact that the present supply of ministers and missionaries falls so far short of the demand? In the voice that comes to us from nation after nation clamouring for the gospel, may we not hear a providential summons to peculiar faithfulness in duty towards the rising generation of the church? When we shall have realized a higher standard of fidelity in discharging this important trust, the church and the family engaging hand in hand in their common work of training souls for eternity, and rearing a seed for God, it will be found that there is a tremendous power for good in this too much neglected class of obligations; and that the covenant, "I will be a God to thee, and to thy seed after thee,"—which probably has never yet been understood in its glorious fulness of meaning—affords the true basis for the extension and final triumph of the Redeemer's kingdom in the world.

CHAPTER IX.

THE VALUE, DIFFICULTIES, AND AIDS OF FAMILY RELIGION.

I. Its value.—The zeal with which we labour for any proposed end is generally proportioned to our estimate of its value. Whatever men exalt in their minds to the dignity of a *chief good*, whether it be wealth, fame, pleasure, or the soul's salvation, is sure to engage their earnest efforts for its attainment. For this reason, all argument in favour of the *duty* of religion in the family may prove comparatively powerless with those who regard it as of trifling value, while they who realize its worth will strive vigorously to secure it. Although, therefore, this part of our subject has been in part anticipated, we may profitably attend to a few thoughts bearing upon it.

It may be remarked, in general, that *whatever renders religion a blessing to the individual, makes it the same to the family.* Look at some of its characteristic features. Does it tend to the fulfilment of the purpose for which man was created? So, also, as has been shown, it promotes the end of the family constitution. Does it make man virtuous and holy in heart and life? It likewise secures the virtue and purity of the family that it governs. Does it promote our happiness, by sanctifying the enjoyments and trials of life? It affords also the only enduring basis for domestic bliss, and while sweetening the joys of the family, furnishes a solace for its griefs. Does it crown the hopes of the believer with boundless and eternal pleasures in heaven? So, too, when thoroughly pervading the household, it at last gathers all its members to the heavenly home.

The godless family is liable to many forms of misery from which there is no relief save that which religion furnishes. With all its endearing ties and beautiful affections, still, like the death's head at the ancient feasts, sin is ever present to mar and embitter them. Witness the various phases of selfishness, the occasional outbreaks of passion, envy, and uncharitableness, the acts of disobedience to parental authority, and the general impatience of wholesome restraints, that pervade many a home that is destitute of religious influences. It may not be without its joys, but is there not mingled with them a consciousness that *one* important element of happiness is wanting, which can be supplied from no earthly source? that something is yet needed to bind heart with heart in closer and more sacred sympathy—some governing principle that shall be the law of the household, guiding its duties and enjoyments, and consecrating them to noble and worthy ends? In an especial manner does this felt want impress itself *in the hour of trouble.* What spectacle, for instance, can be more dismal than that presented by the irreligious family when, returned from the fresh grave of a member, they gaze upon the vacant chair, and think of the hushed voice, whose tones shall never more greet their ears: and yet have no hope of rejoining the departed one in an upper household, and no consoling influences of the Comforter to blunt the edge of grief!

Now mark the home where piety exerts its gentle sway. The ties of nature are strengthened by those of grace, and kindred hearts beat with a holier sympathy because they are one in Christ, and "members one of another." A common faith and hope sweetens all their intercourse, and adds a zest to the daily round of duty. The animating Spirit of God brings forth his appropriate "fruit" of "love, joy, peace, long-suffering, gentleness, goodness, faith, meekness, temperance." And steadily, surely, the Christian family works out its appointed purpose, and renders its perpetual tribute to the Divine glory. While the unsanctified household, like a wandering star, strays from its orbit, that which is governed by religion is kept by it within its appointed sphere, and revolves harmoniously about the "central sun" of God's moral universe, the throne of the Redeemer. Bright and beautiful is its pathway, lit up with the smile of God; and if clouds do sometimes obscure its horizon, they are gilded by rays of infinite love. The holiest domestic scene is not wholly free from sin's ravages. Even the family at Bethany, who were favoured with the peculiar friendship and society of Jesus, were called to endure the anguish of bereavement. Yet how wonderfully does religion rob sorrow of its sting, and smooth the brow of care!

Does adversity threaten? Parents and children study together the word of promise, and faith triumphs over anxiety and distrust as they read, "Never have I seen the righteous forsaken, nor his seed begging bread." Does the hand of disease fasten upon a loved form, wasting its strength and beauty? A holy place is the chamber of sickness, when its occupant is a follower of the Lord Jesus; for religion makes it not so much the verge of the grave as the threshold of heaven. Its walls may echo many a sigh, but the submissive tribute also goes up, "Thy will be done!"—and when the dreaded blow falls on the stricken group, it falls not like a thunderbolt, crushing every hope, and filling all hearts with terror, but like the gentle summer cloud that descends with a blessing in its bosom. "*It is the Lord,*" goes from lip to lip, and the sad parting only quickens the efforts, and renews the diligence of those that remain, that they may not fail to greet the departed in the home and family above.

But not only does religion constitute the only true happiness of the family; it also, and as a necessary means to that end, secures its *fidelity in duty.* It makes better parents, more dutiful children, more faithful husbands and wives, more kind and affectionate brothers and sisters. It gives sanction to parental authority, and efficacy to its example and instruction; imparts the spirit of reverence and obedience to the minds of the young; and clothes with success the whole system of means that are employed in rearing them for the Lord. This it does by affording the most powerful motives to right conduct upon the part of each and every member of the household. Let a parent be animated by no higher aims than this world affords, and he can scarcely resist the temptation to sacrifice moral duty to temporal interest, and to be faithless in the discharge of those obligations which in any way conflict with his views of worldly aggrandizement. For instance, we cannot look for correct instruction and discipline upon the part of one who listens rather to the voice of custom than that of God, and who had rather see his children applauded by fashion's votaries, than by the Judge of quick and dead. So, too, he whose whole course of life is bent towards the accumulation of earthly riches, is ill qualified to point his children, either by word or example, to "treasures in heaven." Upon the other hand, the child, who has no motive for obedience other than the parent's word of authority, or the fear of chastisement, is more likely to rebel against him, than the one whose mind is plied with the incentives of piety, and the commands of God. We are forced to the conclusion that if we would rightly discharge the duties or enjoy the comforts of the family, it must be through the instrumentality of religion. Its worth, therefore, can only be measured by the worth of the family when rightly conducted, and by the endless results of blessedness which it is intended, in the mind of its Originator, to work out.

A slight view of those *results* will show that the value of family religion is far beyond the power of the human mind to conceive or of pen to describe. For, in its true idea, as influencing every member, and including both parents and children in the ark of the covenant, it is nothing less than *family salvation!* This is its object, and this, when it fulfils its whole mission, is its fruit. What a stupendous blessing!—the enclosing of the whole domestic circle in the arms of saving mercy, all being washed in the blood of Christ, and renewed by the Holy Spirit, and together made "meet to be partakers of the inheritance of the saints in light!" If he is not profited who "gains the whole world and loses his soul," how vast must be the worth of a *family of souls*, all saved from wrath and made co-heirs of endless life! Eternity alone can teach us what a priceless treasure those parents possess who open wide their homes and their hearts to the appeals of piety; and who, by God's blessing upon their labours, are the means of adding all the children whom God has given them as jewels to the Saviour's crown. Imagine the blissful scene which is no doubt in reserve for many a "household of faith" in the heavenly world, of the glorified parent standing in the midst of a happy group whom he had led with earnest prayers and counsels to the mansions above, exclaiming, as when upon earth they surrounded the family altar after a night of slumber, "*we are all here!*" "Behold, here am I and the children whom God hath given me." And in the new wave of grateful melody that sweeps from their harps of gold to the throne of the Redeemer, you may hear a tribute, which all eternity will not exhaust, to the value of *religion in the family*.

II. Its Difficulties.—The remark is often made, that it is very easy to theorize upon the subject of family duties and responsibilities, but exceedingly difficult to put our theories in practice. So far as this statement holds good in regard to every class of moral obligations, we cannot deny its applicability to this one. It is always easier to prescribe duty than faithfully to discharge it,—"easier to preach than to practise." Yet it remains to be proved that the difficulties of family religion are any greater than those that beset the application of religion to any other sphere of life. Certainly they are not so vast or insuperable as to be for a moment compared with what we have seen to be its value.

1. One of its chief difficulties is found in *the temptations that are peculiar to the home and fireside.* What engrossing cares—what frequent trials of temper and of patience—what a succession of trivial disturbances to the even tenor of duty,—and what absorbing pleasures, mark this little world! Is it possible, it may be asked, to maintain under such circumstances that calm and equable frame of mind which characterizes true piety? Is not the task of contending against this combination of adverse influences, well nigh hopeless? We candidly admit that it is no slight thing to carry out the demands of religion in the face of so many temptations, and that the family who would follow Christ must, like the individual disciple, deny itself, and take up its cross. It is to be expected that the enemy of souls will intrude into that spot where characters are formed and habits moulded, and that he will not permit human hearts, in that period when they are the most susceptible to good or evil influences, to be wrested from him without a struggle. He therefore presses his warfare amid the sanctities of the domestic circle, and makes of even the Christian home a battle-ground whose every inch he disputes with our Maker. He gives to its cares a distracting charac-

ter, and would trouble the parent about the "many things" that may seem lawfully to engage his attention, until, like Martha, he forgets the "*one thing*" that "*is needful.*"

Yet this difficulty is by no means as formidable as may appear to the casual observer. The very trials incident to the family relation may be made to *subserve*, instead of retard, its spiritual interests, provided only that they be sanctified by piety, and pervaded by the spirit of the gospel. Besides this, none will contend that the obstacles to religion are nearly as great in the bosom of the family, as they are in the world without. Difficult as may seem the task of exerting right influences over the child in his home, is it not far more so to wield them over the mind that has become entangled in the excitements of mature life? Granting, therefore, the alleged obstacles to exist, even to a greater degree than is claimed by any, it is still the part of wisdom to use every endeavour to overcome them, for the reason that they will rather augment than diminish by the lapse of years.

Perhaps one reason why they are not oftener overcome may be found in the *partial efforts* which many are satisfied to put forth. There are those who think to compromise with this class of difficulties, imagining that it will be easier to achieve a half way victory over them, than one that is more complete. Nothing, however, is to be gained by attempts at dividing the burden of religious obligation with the world. Let the most thorough, pervasive piety be aimed at—one that shall extend to the trifles of each passing moment, equally with events of magnitude, and that shall be woven into the web of daily life, influencing alike the grave cares of the parent, and the petty trials of the child; and, as we proceed, these obstacles will one by one vanish, or be converted by sanctifying grace into valuable aids to the work with which they had seemingly conflicted. Strength is gained by repeated and hard fought victories, and piety in the family, as in the individual, obtains a stronger hold, and shines with a brighter lustre, for the very obstacles with which it has had to contend.

One of the most common difficulties in the way of family religion, arising from the source under consideration, is thus ably presented by Rev. Dr. Nehemiah Adams, in his work on "The Communion Sabbath." "The distance between members of the same family with regard to religious conversation and communion—the common saying and feeling, 'I can talk with every one else more freely than I can with those of my own family,' is owing very much to consciousness of inconsistency in little things which is recognized at home, and to those little differences, or faults, or trespasses which make the thought of communing together in spiritual things repulsive. Strangers do not know these easily-besetting sins. But if we, members of the same family, seek sweet counsel together; if brothers, if sisters would accustom themselves to pray together; if during some heavy calamity which has fallen on the house, or under the influence of some great blessing, they should begin this practice, and while their hearts are under the subduing influences of sorrow or joy, they should together seek God, and become attached as Christians by such communion with each other and with Christ, these petty inconsistencies would be greatly prevented; there would be Christian friendship in families, beautiful and strong; and that sad distance and alienation which too often exists among the children of a family, and extends through life, would be exchanged for that unity which is described by inspiration as 'good and pleasant.'"

2. Another frequent source of difficulty is found in *the want of coöperation upon the part of some member of the family.*

Instances are by no means rare, in which either the father or mother is compelled to labour alone for the attainment of this end. Here is a serious obstacle. The position of the Christian parent who has not the sympathy and assistance of his or her companion in this work, is sad in the extreme, and greatly to be commiserated. Especially hard does it seem, when the irreligious parent openly opposes the other's efforts, and by both counsel and example endeavours to thwart them. Here, truly, is need of strong faith and earnest resolution. Can family religion be secured under such adverse influences?

This difficulty, so far from discouraging the parent, ought rather to redouble those efforts which God is accustomed to bless to the end in view. The want of human sympathy and coöperation should drive us the more closely to the throne and the heart of Jesus, and deepen our sense of dependence upon God. Especially should it incite to persevering endeavours for the conversion of the irreligious one, and the enlisting of his or her example upon the side of piety. The task may be arduous and protracted, yet if crowned, as in many instances it is, with success, it for that very reason issues in a purer and holier joy. So far as regards the offspring of a family thus divided, God graciously enfolds them in the covenant with his people, and does not permit the unbelief of the one parent to deprive them of the benefits of the other's faith. Thus Paul declares, "The unbelieving husband is sanctified by the wife, and the unbelieving wife is sanctified by the husband; else were your children unclean," (*i. e.*, without the pale of the church,) "but now are they holy," (*i. e.*, consecrated, sustaining a relation to God and his church.) 1 Cor. vii. 14. The believing parent, then, who is so situated, may still plead the promise of the covenant in regard to his children, and pray for their conversion in the faith that it will be granted.

Instances are not unfrequent in which such faith has been crowned with signal success. Often has the devoted mother, toiling and praying for years, alone and single handed, been permitted to see one and another of her children, and the partner of her life, enfolded in the flock of the good Shepherd. And here we cannot but remark that of those parents who are divided upon the subject of religion, the piety is generally upon the side of *the mother*—a circumstance which we may regard as not wholly without design; for it is the mother who, in the early and more susceptible years of childhood, wields the most powerful influence, and who possesses the most favourable opportunities for directing the mind towards heaven.

A beautiful triumph of faith over this kind of discouragement is related of a mother who was for many years the only Christian in the family, her husband and nine children giving no evidence of piety. Instead of yielding to the current, under the plea that resistance would be unavailing, she felt that God had committed to her trust *ten* unconverted souls; and that if any were lost, it should not be through her neglect of duty. She aimed, first of all, at leading a holy, consistent life, and also improved every opportunity for instruction and tender warning. Her chief reliance, however, was upon fervent, believing prayer. She presented each child separately before the throne of grace, and in due time, she prevailed with God. The first convert was her eldest daughter; the two eldest sons followed soon after; and successively the whole of the nine children made a profession of faith. Yet amid all the grateful joy of that mother's heart, one sorrow for a season remained—the husband and father was still impenitent. He was now advancing in years, and had begun to form the habit of intemperance. Might not his harvest be past? The faithful wife resolved upon one final effort. After a night of anguished supplication, she plead once more with her husband, reminded him of her many prayers for him, of their children's conversion, and of his probable separation from her in eternity—adding, "*Do, this moment, seek the salvation of your soul!*" He replied with significant emphasis, "I *will!*" and in a few days that family circle was complete in Christ, for the father had passed "from death unto life." "The praying mother still lives," continues the narrator of this incident; "she has seen her children connected with pious families, and listened to some of them as preachers of the gospel. Most of her grand-children are members of the church, one a missionary to a foreign land, and for each of the unconverted she continues the daily prayer."

Let none, then, regard this difficulty as insuperable, or hesitate to grapple with it, in reliance upon infinite grace. Faith can remove even this "mountain." "*With God all things are possible.*"

3. Not to specify other and lesser difficulties that are involved in the attainment of the end in view, we may include them all under one, *the depravity and opposition of the human heart.*

It is this that opposes the great barrier to religion, whether in the individual, society, or the race at large, and into this, at last, every other obstacle must be resolved. It causes the commands of God to grate upon the unsanctified ear; it arrays the heart against him who would bless it with his love; it gives to the world its charm, to sin its sweetness, and to piety its fancied gloom. It lies at the root of both parental and filial unfaithfulness, and until it be eradicated by converting grace, effectually opposes the end of the family relation.

Man has no natural relish for piety. Even the little child, in all his comparative innocence and purity, is averse to it, and his heart is "enmity against God." Here, then, in the very nature of the beings whom we endeavour to influence, lies the most formidable hinderance to the duties which we have contemplated. If regarded from a merely human point of view, it is not only difficult to overcome this—it is impossible. No instrumentality that is less than Divine can conform the hearts of old or young to the dictates of religion. Yet to those who faithfully employ the allotted means, and especially that of fervent prayer, is given the promise of an Almighty power, that is stronger than our depravity and rebellion, and which engages to second our efforts and crown them with success.

This greatest of all difficulties, then, is one that may be surmounted. And this being the case, what is there left to stagger our faith, or paralyze our efforts? For, if Divine grace be at hand to renew the sinful soul, and make it a "new creature" in Christ Jesus, it surely is equal to the removal of all lesser obstacles to piety in the family. The power that can convert a child of wrath, in answer to believing prayer, can readily remove the most powerful hinderances to its conversion, can overcome the example of an irreligious parent or friend, can drown the voice of the world, and of temptation, can counteract all adverse influences, and enable the Christian successfully to combat them.

Thus does our view of the root of all difficulties upon this subject, remind us of the source of all power wherewith to contend with them. There is, then, no reason for discouragement. Faith may be tried, and the heart sometimes despond, and circumstances may appear peculiarly unfavourable to our hopes, but let the Christian rest upon the sure word of promise, and derive courage from on high. Let him look rather at duty than at difficulty, and at the blessed result rather than the arduous means, and he need never despair.

"Faith, precious faith, the promise sees,
And looks at that alone;
Laughs at impossibilities,
And cries, *It shall be done.*"

III. Its aids.—While the enemy of all religion is heaping obstacles in the way of its practice, its Divine Author affords us many aids towards discharging its duties and securing its blessings. The different *means* provided to this end have already been noticed. It only remains that we specify some valuable auxiliaries which come more appropriately under our present head of discussion.

1. One of these is *a careful attention to the early habits of the family.*

These are to a great degree under the control of the parent, and should ever be made to harmonize with the requirements of religion. Thus, children may early be accustomed to pray, to read the Scriptures, to attend upon family worship, and upon the services of the sanctuary,—all of which will tend powerfully towards keeping the claims of God before their minds, and impressing them with their importance. Upon the other hand, if carelessly permitted to grow up in the neglect of these duties, it will be difficult to habituate them to their observance in after years. We are all "creatures of habit," and God does not often reverse that principle of our constitution which makes us such, but requires that we improve it in furtherance of the spiritual interests of ourselves and others. Constant care is requisite, in order to render it conducive to this end upon the part of the family; for, as every one is aware, it is far more difficult to conquer wrong habits than to form right ones at the outset.

The Christian parent, therefore, should carefully watch over his children in this respect. Regarding them in their true character as members of the church, and as consecrated to the Divine service, he should guard against their indulgence in any thing that is inconsistent with this solemn relationship, or prejudicial to true piety. For instance, what a blow is inflicted upon the moral character of the child or youth who is thoughtlessly permitted to associate with evil companions, and to join in their career of idleness or dissipation! What probability is there of serious impressions being retained for any length of time by those who frequent the giddy dancing-school, the soul-enervating ball-room, the demoralizing circus, or the theatre! The practice of attending upon such places is generally formed, and the taste for them acquired, while under the eye of the parent; and a judicious exercise of authority will generally suffice to turn the mind to more wholesome and legitimate sources of entertainment. Many a one who has fallen a victim to parental indifference, has bitterly lamented that he was not more carefully guarded upon this point; and in some instances, perhaps in many, dying souls have attributed their perdition to the mistaken kindness which indulged their youthful follies. Says a venerable divine, "I was called in the early part of my ministry to stand beside the bed of a beautiful young mother, whose life was fast ebbing away. Anguish, deep, hopeless anguish was riveted on her countenance. I asked her if she was willing that I should pray with her. Her reply was, 'I have no objection, but prayers will be of no avail now; it is too late, too late; *I must die; I am lost! lost for ever!'* I prayed earnestly with her, but her hard heart was untouched; there was in it no fountain of love to its Maker, and it was 'too late.' She had been, at a very early period of life, seriously impressed, 'but,' said she, '*my mother sent me to the dancing-school, and I danced all my convictions away.*' As she lived, so did she die,—without Christ in the world."

It may seem a trifling matter to allow a child *for once* to mingle in the society of the wicked and profane, or to taste the tempting wine, or to visit scenes of unchristian amusement; but let the parent reflect that it is more difficult to prevent the second step than the first, and that the child whose principles are not yet matured, and whose impulses have not been modified by experience, will quickly acquire those habits which may yet master him, body and soul, and ruin his prospects for eternity.

> "The clay is moist and soft; now, now make haste,
> And form the pitcher, for the wheel turns fast."

And "the pitcher, once formed, may be more easily broken than altered."

2. As an important aid towards securing family religion, diligent attention should be paid to *the reading of the family.*

The present age is prolific in literature for the young; and while furnishing much that is of a good tendency, it also provides a great deal whose influence is only evil. The character of books intended for the nursery has, of late years, changed greatly for the better; yet the wild romances of past generations, founded upon scenes that are not only imaginary but impossible, still form, to too great an extent, the standard tales of childhood. It appears to be taken for granted in them that the infant mind is capable only of being amused, not instructed, and that there can be no harm in filling it with mere figments of the imagination—things that never existed, and scenes that could never have occurred.

Yet, is it no injury to the child to be entertained with tales which have no correspondence with real life, and which only excite and feed a morbid imagination? Is it not a serious thing for the sentiment of truthfulness to receive such early and repeated shocks, and for the child to be led to believe that he must go beyond the actual world to a kind of dream-land, filled with ghosts, giants, and hobgoblins, for his mind's proper food? Says Dr. Thomas Dick, "When the young mind is just beginning to expand, instead of being irradiated with the beams of unadulterated truth, a group of distorted and unsubstantial images, which have no prototypes in nature, is presented to the view of the intellect, as the groundwork of its future progress in wisdom and knowledge." After enumerating a few of them, such as Blue Beard, Cinderella, Tom Thumb, Jack the Giant Killer, etc., the same author proceeds: "And what are the great objects they are calculated to accomplish? To exhibit distorted views of human nature and of society, to foster superstition, to inspire the minds of the young with an inordinate desire after worldly honour and distinction, to set before them as an ultimate object the splendour of riding in a coach and six, and to familiarize their minds with chivalrous exploits, and scenes of butchery and revenge."

Happily, the present generation of children are not dependent upon this worthless nursery literature. Christian writers have vied with each other in ministering to their amusement in a way that shall profit instead of demoralizing them, and attractive books are at hand which the parent may safely place before the young, with no fear of injury either to their minds or morals.

At least equal care should be taken to provide healthful and instructive reading for *those who have passed the years of childhood.* The press teems with a class of works whose influence is highly prejudicial to a right mental or moral culture upon the part of their readers. Most of the popular novels of the day are a fruitful source of injury to those who indulge in their perusal, and ought to be banished from every family which recognizes the Bible as its law. Besides their enervating effect upon the mind, and their unhealthy excitement of the imagination, they are apt to beget a familiarity with crime, and a false sympathy with the criminal and the vicious. They also excite wrong views of life, and tend to disqualify their readers for its grave realities. Worse than all, they are apt to exalt the dreams of fiction above the pure truths of revelation, and to give a distaste for the pages of the "Book of books." Like every other wrong habit, this one has been known to lead its votaries to ruin. By frequent indulgence it grows to be a passion as strong and irresistible as that of the drunkard for his cups, or the gambler for his cards. An instance was recently brought to light in which the misery and destitution of an entire family in England was clearly traced by the authorities to the ungovernable passion of the wife and mother for *novel reading*. Though the husband was sober and industrious, the wife thus became indolent and neglectful of her family, until one daughter fled from home and entered the haunts of vice, while another was found by the police, chained in the house, to prevent her from following her sister's example. And there, in the midst of filth and indigence, sat this cause of it, reading the latest "sensation book" of the season!

Such is its tendency. It is a foe to the healthful action of the mind or heart, an enemy to peace, and especially to religion. Let the parent guard his children at this point, and place in their hands judicious selections from religious and instructive literature; and while not denying them occasional works of an entertaining character, let them be such as are not unprofitable. A proper attention to the wants of the family in this particular will assist materially in the preservation of correct morals, and the prevalence of religion among its members.

3. Another powerful aid to the Christian parent is *the Sabbath-school.*

While affording no substitute for the instructions of the fireside, this is yet, when rightly improved, a most powerful auxiliary to them. It provides a thorough and systematic course of instruction in sacred truth, under circumstances that are peculiarly calculated to interest the youthful mind. The holy day, the assembled numbers, the concert of study and recitation, the chorus of childish voices joining in appropriate hymns, and the kind words of the beloved teacher—all combine to invest the Sabbath-school with powerful attractions. Most children learn to love it as one of their chief pleasures, and look forward to it with impatience. Whether it shall accomplish its end in them or not, depends much upon their parents. The most faithful teacher, who is deprived of their coöperation, labours under a great disadvantage. Care should therefore be taken that children be prepared at home for deriving the utmost benefit from this institution.

The history of the Sabbath-school in this country has amply demonstrated its value as a help to the appropriate work of the Christian family. It has been blessed to the conversion of large multitudes of the rising generation, both of those born within and without the pale of the church. So manifestly does it bear the stamp of the Divine approval, and so general is the recognition of its usefulness, that it requires no lengthened advocacy at our hands. It is perhaps enough for our purpose to name it, and pass on.

Other aids to the object before us might be suggested, but they will readily occur to one who earnestly engages in the duties of the family relation. Every proper and legitimate means of influence should be seized upon, and made tributary to religion. Slight aids ought not to be overlooked, nor should anything be deemed trivial that tends to promote so valuable an end. The little hymn, learned at a mother's knee, may furnish material for many a serious reflection. The verse of Scripture, recited, as was the commendable practice of the early Christians, at the morning meal, may afford solace for a dying hour.

We know not what means God may bless, and therefore it only remains that we diligently improve them all:

> "And as the bird each fond endearment tries,
> To tempt her new-fledged offspring to the skies;
> Employ each art; reprove each dull delay;
> Allure to brighter worlds, and lead the way."

CHAPTER X.

PLEAS FOR NEGLECT AND DELINQUENCIES, DISCUSSED AND REFUTED.

In view of the importance and binding character of family religion, it might safely be assumed that no plea can justify its neglect. The bare fact that it is enjoined by Him who has the right to impose it, would seem to be enough to answer every objection, and to leave its neglecter without excuse. For the most plausible of pretexts cannot divest the evasion of these duties of its true character of *disobedience to God.* Yet as, in our Lord's day, those bidden to the gospel feast "began with one consent to make excuse," it is not surprising that there should now be those who claim an exemption from the obligations and privileges that have passed in review before us. Let us notice a few of the most common pleas for such delinquency.

1. It is affirmed by some that *the burden of worldly cares* renders it impossible for them to attend to the religious interests of the household. It is necessary, say they, that we provide for the temporal wants of those

dependent upon us, and if we do this, no time is left for promoting their spiritual good.

Fully admitting the necessity of those anxieties and toils that relate to the sustenance of the family, we still ask whether at least an equal necessity does not exist for their being supplied with *the soul's* proper food; and whether there is any warrant for thus sacrificing the spiritual to the corporeal, and the eternal to the temporal? What would be thought of the parent who should permit his family to suffer hunger, cold, and nakedness, upon the plea that he must provide for their wants as moral beings, and has no time left in which to feed and clothe their bodies? Such an instance, it may be said, was never known to exist; yet when we contrast the value of the spiritual with that of the temporal, ought we not to conclude that if either interest must suffer, it ought rather to be the latter than the former?

There is, however, no need of their thus conflicting; and we should beware how we thus charge our neglect of duty upon the providence of God. It may be questioned whether any care which really hinders the parent in his appointed work is not *self-imposed*, and, so far as it tends to the neglect of higher obligations, unwarranted. For instance, God nowhere requires that we expend our time and strength in order to secure the mere luxuries of life, or to meet the demands of fashionable extravagance, or to maintain a certain social position; but *he does require* that we train our children "in the nurture and admonition of the Lord," and that we meet the demands of the family constitution. And can there be any question as to which class of obligations is the highest, those of worldly custom, or the law of God? It is, however, rather the excess of warrantable cares that is urged in justification of this neglect, and herein consists the chief plausibility of the plea. How, it is asked, can the father, who toils early and late to earn bread for his children, or the mother, busied in constant household duties, be expected to devote much attention to the claims of piety in the family?

This, it must be admitted, is at first sight a serious difficulty; and we cannot withhold the tribute of sympathy from those who labour under it. Yet observation will show that, so far from its being insurmountable, religion generally shines the most brightly in that class of families whose circumstances allow them but little leisure, while the home that is marked by freedom from worldly anxiety seems not thereby to be in a state any the more favourable to piety. In fact, a proper degree of industry is an important requisite of religion, and tends much more to the development of an earnest Christian character than a life of indolence. In addition to this, let it be borne in mind that the tendency of religion is rather to lighten than increase the burden of care, and this plea for its neglect becomes a powerful *argument in its favour.*

2. A common plea for neglecting one of the most important of these duties is, "*I cannot pray in my family.* I am too diffident," or, "I have not time," or "I cannot conduct such an exercise to edification."

Yet, are such as would thus excuse themselves, too timid to ask others for that which will promote the *temporal* good of their children? Or does their modesty ever form a bar to social enjoyment? And what is there, we ask, in his own household, that should cause the parent to shrink from leading them in daily devotion? If it is the fear of criticism, the dread that his children or friends will sit in judgment upon his words, this is but an ignoble motive to sway a Christian man, and deter him, day after day, from acknowledged duty. Such a one may rather blush at the weakness which he thus displays, and the dishonour thus reflected upon the name that he professes. The fear of God ought certainly to preponderate over the fear of man, and, viewed in its true aspect, it savours more of pride than humility to make use of this frequent plea. Much as any may fear to undertake the duty of family worship, they should be still more afraid to neglect it. All can pray to God who can converse with their friends; and though the petition be not always clothed in the most polished diction, it may yet express acceptably the heart's earnest longings, and become that "effectual, fervent prayer," which "availeth much."

Were this excuse to be applied, as with equal reason it might be, to other branches of religious duty, to what consequences would it lead us? With no less propriety it might deter the preacher from opening his lips in the pulpit, and might seal the voice of the Christian in the prayer meeting, or in conversation with the ungodly, and of the teacher in the Sabbath-school. It is a temptation of the adversary, and as such should be strenuously resisted and overcome. The chief difficulty lies in the *first effort*. If this be resolutely made, in reliance upon infinite grace, the parent will soon find that which he had so long dreaded, to be an easy and delightful task.

The plea of a *want of time* for this and kindred duties, requires only a passing notice. For, why is time given us, if not that it may be improved for the divine glory in promoting the end of our existence, whether as individuals or as families? Every precious moment, as it comes and goes, is the gift of God, and to him it should be consecrated. He does indeed afford us hours for toil, and needed relaxation, but we have no right to appropriate it *all* to selfish purposes. To do this, is to rob our Maker of his own, and to rob our families, and indeed ourselves, of inestimable blessings. That time cannot be called gained, but it is rather lost, which is stolen from the claims of religion. There is deep significance in the saying of Matthew Henry, "Prayers and provender never hinder a journey."

3. The plea is sometimes urged, *that there are instances of the conversion of children without any special effort upon the part of their parents.*

That God is pleased, in some cases, to avert the disastrous consequences of wrong doing, affords no palliation for that wrong. Such, however, is not the *ordinary method* of the Divine government. Where he has connected a certain means with a given end, he teaches us that we can only *expect* that end in the use of the appointed means. Most remarkably is this principle illustrated in the family. It is governed by natural laws, which are not unlike those of seed-time and harvest, one of which is, "Whatsoever a man soweth, that shall he also reap." And the young heart is a field in which the parent is always sowing seed of one kind or another. He cannot help doing so; and if by his active efforts he do not implant the good seed, he is, by his very neglect, sowing thorns and thistles, and the harvest will be accordingly. He therefore runs a fearful risk who wastes and perverts the spring-time of those entrusted to him, in the vague hope that God *may* yet make amends for his negligence. Certainly such have no warrant for the faith that their children will be converted, but have every reason to expect the contrary.

4. Others adduce a plea of an opposite character in justification of parental neglect, namely, *that the greatest faithfulness sometimes fails of its end.*

We hesitate not to affirm that the truth of this assertion has never been proved. To say that the children of those who were eminently pious do sometimes become open and bold transgressors, does not establish it; for until it be shown that their piety was not deficient in the particular of home duties, the whole course of the Divine government warrants us in maintaining that their ill success is chargeable rather to themselves than God. It is not always the piety that attracts the most attention abroad, that exerts the most influence in the family. While we would not be understood as pronouncing harsh judgment upon any, we may be permitted to suggest that the very activity in outward religious duties which commands public attention and admiration, is sometimes practised at the expense of those pertaining to the family. The Christian parent may be unconscious of his mistake, and animated only by worthy and conscientious motives; yet it will be seen that that which renders him prominent as a Christian may thus be the reason of a negligence in the discharge of home obligations, which will sufficiently account for the sinful career of his children. These two classes of duty need not, indeed, conflict, yet the fact that they sometimes do, will be evident to every careful observer, and will afford a sufficient reason for the ill-success in their homes, of some who are esteemed "eminent" in piety.

There is an old cavil which is often repeated, to the effect that *ministers' and deacons' children do not generally follow in the footsteps of their fathers.* Happily, this has been refuted by the most conclusive evidence. A gentleman who was anxious to arrive at the truth upon this much vexed subject, took pains to collect voluminous statistics, of which the following is the published result: "In two hundred and forty-one families of ministers and deacons, there were eleven hundred and sixty-four children over fifteen years of age. Of these children, eight hundred and fourteen—*more than three-fourths*—were hopefully pious; seven hundred and thirty-two had united with the church; fifty-seven had entered the ministry, or were engaged in their preparatory studies; and *only fourteen* were dissipated, about one-half of whom only became so while residing with their parents. In twenty-seven of those families, there were one hundred twenty-three children, all of whom but seven were hopefully pious; seven of them were deacons, and fifteen ministers. In fifty-six of those families, there were two hundred and forty-nine children over fifteen years of age, and *all were hopefully pious.*" To this may be added the testimony of Dr. Sprague's "Annals of the American Pulpit."

Of the sons of one hundred ministers whose lives he has recorded, *over one hundred and ten* became ministers.

The case of Aaron Burr, whose parents and grandparents were eminently pious, has sometimes been quoted as a dark and mysterious one. For many years the history of that profligate "child of the covenant" seemed almost to stagger the faith of some who were familiar with it, and to afford strong warrant for the plea we are now considering. But mark how in this instance, which was becoming historic, God interposed to vindicate his faithfulness. The testimony of the eldest son of President Edwards, which we have already introduced in another connection,* has within a few years come to light, and shown conclusively that Burr, who was early left an orphan, was "suffered to grow up" undisciplined, and without that government and training which God's word enjoins as indispensable to parental faithfulness.

In view of the foregoing facts and considerations, the strongest warrant is afforded us for *expecting* a blessing upon fidelity in the family. Parental faithfulness is, indeed, never what it should be, and we have as frequent need of the Divine forgiveness for our short-comings in this, as in other respects. Yet God bears with our infirmities, assists our feeble efforts, and generally guides them to a happy issue. True, he does sometimes try his people's faith by delaying the blessing, but he does not therefore forget his covenant. For mysterious reasons, he may permit the parent to die with his prayers unanswered; yet even then he can sustain his hopes that the answer will not always be deferred.

---

* Page 50.

A remarkable instance of faith thus triumphing over discouragement was narrated by the late Dr. Archibald Alexander. Conversing with an aged Christian, an elder, upon the efficacy of prayer, the old man informed him that his eldest son, who was a lawyer of some eminence, and of unblemished moral character, was yet unconcerned about his own salvation. "But," said he, "I have had such nearness to God, and such liberty in prayer for his conversion, that I believe those prayers will be answered in due time, whether I live to see it or not." Soon afterwards the old elder was gathered to his fathers. The son of so many prayers fell into habits of intemperance, and "in fact, became a mere sot, remaining at home and stupefying himself with alcoholic drinks every day. Such a case," continues the narrator, "appeared to me nearly hopeless. I have seldom known a man thus brought under the power of strong drink to recover himself. * * * But, behold the truth and faithfulness of a prayer-hearing God. This man, after continuing in intemperate habits until the age of seventy or more, became completely reclaimed; and not only delivered from that vice, but converted to God. He not only gave evidence of a change, but appeared to be eminent in the practice of piety. At this time he was about eighty years of age. How wonderful are the ways of God! His faithfulness never faileth; it reacheth unto the clouds. 'Thy faithfulness is *unto all generations!*' "

We have characterized this instance as remarkable,—yet, after all, is it not in keeping with the known course of God's dealings with his people? The history of the church abounds in attestations of the same divine faithfulness as rewarding a proper degree of fidelity upon the part of Christian parents, and affords all the encouragement that the most trembling heart could desire, to labour and pray for religion in the family.

In refuting the plea before us, then, we are legitimately conducted to a powerful motive to earnest confidence and hope. "He is faithful that hath promised, who also will do it." Cast thyself, O parent, upon the sure word of Jehovah! Let faith take strong hold of the covenant, for it is "well ordered in all things, *and sure!*" Endeavouring fully to realize the vastness of the blessing and the divine efficacy of the means, aim at the utmost diligence in that work which surpasses every other in importance,—the training of immortal souls for the Divine service and glory,—"forasmuch as ye know that your labour is not in vain in the Lord." We live in a dying world. We are all, whether parents or children, but "pilgrims and strangers" in the earth. Time flies apace, and swiftly bears us beyond these scenes of present duty. Let it be so improved that the union of loved hearts upon earth shall be typical of a closer and more holy fellowship hereafter. Then, though there be sad partings, as one by one the family is transferred to the upper household, the separation shall be but temporary,—the reunion eternal.

Precious and delightful are those scenes that often occur in the earthly family, when its scattered members meet in some dear old homestead, from which some of them have long been separated, and hold sweet intercourse together; but far more blissful will be the final gathering of the Christian family in the upper home, when neither father nor mother, son nor daughter shall be absent, but their voices shall blend in anthems of praise, and hand be linked in hand as they tread the banks of the "river of the water of life," never more to be parted. Then, amid songs and smiles of rapture shall be seen the culmination and reward of that RELIGION IN THE FAMILY which was here nurtured amid tears and prayers; as, with a holier love than ever before, they worship their common Father, and with a sweeter, richer sympathy than they had known upon earth, delight in one another's companionship, in "the house not made with hands, eternal in the heavens."

www.ingramcontent.com/pod-product-compliance
Lightning Source LLC
LaVergne TN
LVHW011217110826
845150LV00006B/1459

* 9 7 8 1 4 2 5 5 1 6 8 6 4 *